Patch Management and System Updates: Strategies for Stability and Security

James Relington

DEDICATION
To those who seek knowledge, inspiration, and new perspectives—
may this book be a companion on your journey, a spark for curiosity,
and a reminder that every page turned is a step toward discovery.

AKNOWLEDGEMENTS

I would like to express my deepest gratitude to everyone who contributed to the creation of this book. To my colleagues and mentors, your insights and expertise have been invaluable. A special thank you to my family and friends for their unwavering support and encouragement throughout this journey.

Patch Management: The Cornerstone of Security

In the world of cybersecurity, patch management is considered one of the most fundamental practices for ensuring the stability and security of any system or network. Patches are software updates released by vendors to correct vulnerabilities, fix bugs, and improve the performance of programs or systems. The significance of patch management has grown over the years as the threat landscape has evolved. Hackers and malicious actors are constantly on the lookout for vulnerabilities in widely used software and systems, and failing to apply patches in a timely manner can leave organizations exposed to cyber-attacks. The effectiveness of a robust patch management strategy cannot be overstated, as it forms the foundation of an organization's overall security posture.

In its simplest form, patch management involves the identification, acquisition, testing, and deployment of patches to maintain system integrity. This process is not limited to just operating systems but extends to applications, network devices, and any other software that might have vulnerabilities. One of the core reasons patch management is so crucial is that many cyber-attacks exploit known vulnerabilities that have already been patched by the software vendors. When a patch is released, it's typically the result of a security flaw being discovered. These flaws can range from small, insignificant errors to critical vulnerabilities that expose systems to the risk of data breaches, ransomware, or denial-of-service attacks. Without patching these vulnerabilities, the window of opportunity for attackers remains open, which is why timely patch management is essential.

The challenge with patch management, however, is not simply applying patches but ensuring they are applied efficiently and effectively across all systems. In an ideal world, applying patches would be a straightforward process. However, the reality is far more complicated. Organizations are often faced with hundreds or thousands of systems that need to be maintained, and many of these systems may run on different operating systems, applications, or hardware. Furthermore, not all patches are created equal. Some patches address critical security vulnerabilities, while others may focus on improving system functionality or performance. This variance in patch priorities means organizations must carefully assess which patches to apply first, which can be a time-consuming process. The complexity of managing these patches across various environments only intensifies as the size and scope of the organization increase.

Moreover, patch deployment can carry risks. Sometimes patches, particularly those that involve significant changes or updates to systems, can introduce unintended consequences. A patch that fixes one problem might inadvertently create another. For instance, a patch may conflict with existing software, leading to system crashes or application failures. The risk of such issues means that patches must be tested in a controlled environment before being deployed across the enterprise. In addition, some patches may require a system reboot or downtime, which could disrupt business operations. These factors make patch management a balancing act between addressing security vulnerabilities and minimizing operational disruptions.

Another factor that complicates patch management is the rapid pace at which new vulnerabilities are discovered. In recent years, the number of zero-day vulnerabilities—flaws that are exploited before the vendor has had a chance to release a patch—has increased. Zero-day vulnerabilities are particularly dangerous because there is often no immediate solution, leaving systems vulnerable for extended periods. In these cases, organizations need to rely on workarounds or mitigations until a patch is made available. However, this waiting period can result in serious risks if the vulnerability is exploited by attackers during this window.

The role of automation in patch management cannot be overlooked. In today's complex IT environments, where systems and software are constantly being updated, relying solely on manual processes for patch management is impractical and inefficient. Automation tools can streamline the patching process by automatically detecting and deploying patches across systems. These tools can also prioritize patches based on their severity and the potential risks they pose. Additionally, automated patch management systems can provide visibility into which systems are up to date and which ones still require attention, reducing the chances of missed patches. For organizations with large-scale IT infrastructures, automation is not just a convenience—it is a necessity for maintaining security and operational efficiency.

Despite the obvious benefits of patch management, some organizations still face resistance to its implementation. In many cases, this resistance comes from within the organization itself. Some employees or departments may view patch management as a time-consuming task that diverts resources from other pressing priorities. Others may be concerned about the potential disruptions caused by patching. These concerns are valid but can be mitigated through proper planning, testing, and communication. Educating staff about the importance of patch management and its role in preventing security breaches can also help reduce resistance and build a culture of security awareness within the organization.

Another important aspect of patch management is its integration with other security practices. Patch management should not be viewed in isolation. It needs to be a part of a broader security strategy that includes vulnerability management, network monitoring, and incident response. Vulnerability assessments should be conducted regularly to identify systems that need patching, while monitoring tools can alert administrators to any unusual activity that might indicate an attack is underway. When a breach does occur, the ability to quickly identify whether a patch was missing or improperly applied can be crucial in understanding the root cause and preventing future incidents.

In conclusion, patch management is a critical component of any organization's security strategy. Its importance is underscored by the fact that many successful cyber-attacks exploit known vulnerabilities that could have been mitigated through timely patching. A well-managed patching process ensures that vulnerabilities are addressed promptly and effectively, reducing the risk of exploitation and maintaining system integrity. The challenges of patch management are significant, but with the right tools, processes, and a proactive approach, organizations can ensure their systems remain secure and resilient in the face of ever-evolving cyber threats.

The Importance of Regular System Updates

In the fast-evolving world of technology, system updates play a pivotal role in maintaining the security, stability, and functionality of software and hardware systems. While the concept of updating software may seem like a routine process, its importance cannot be overstated. Regular system updates are critical not only for the maintenance of a system's operational performance but also for safeguarding it from the growing landscape of cyber threats. They address vulnerabilities, improve system performance, and ensure compatibility with new technologies. Failure to implement regular updates can lead to significant security risks and operational inefficiencies that can have far-reaching consequences.

The most significant reason for performing regular system updates is the security of the system. Cybercriminals continuously search for weaknesses in operating systems, applications, and devices that they can exploit. These vulnerabilities are often identified by security researchers or, unfortunately, malicious hackers. Once a flaw is discovered, the software vendor typically develops an update or patch to close the vulnerability and prevent potential attacks. If these updates are not applied promptly, systems remain exposed to attackers who can exploit these weaknesses. This can result in data breaches, malware infections, or even complete system takeovers. Regularly updating systems ensures that known vulnerabilities are addressed in a timely manner, reducing the likelihood of a successful cyber-attack.

In addition to fixing security flaws, regular system updates often include enhancements that improve the performance and stability of the system. Over time, software can become outdated or less efficient due to bugs, compatibility issues, or new requirements introduced by evolving hardware or other software. Updates often introduce optimizations that improve system speed, responsiveness, and overall functionality. Without these updates, systems can become sluggish or unstable, negatively affecting user experience and productivity. These performance issues might not be immediately noticeable but can accumulate over time, causing frustration and increasing the likelihood of system failures or crashes.

Another key reason for regular system updates is the need for compatibility with other software and technologies. As the technological landscape continues to evolve, new applications, platforms, and standards emerge. To ensure that systems can interact with these new technologies and integrate seamlessly with other software, updates are often required. This is particularly important in environments that rely on multiple interconnected systems, where one outdated software component can create compatibility problems across the entire infrastructure. Updates ensure that systems remain compatible with the latest versions of operating systems, software libraries, and industry standards, helping organizations avoid integration issues and downtime.

System updates also address usability improvements, which can enhance the user experience. Many updates include new features, user interface improvements, or accessibility enhancements that make systems easier to use and more efficient. These changes might seem minor at first, but they can significantly impact productivity and the overall effectiveness of the system. For example, a software update might include a new feature that streamlines a specific task or adds a shortcut to commonly used functions. These small but important changes can improve workflow, reduce manual effort, and make systems more intuitive for users.

Beyond the individual benefits for users and organizations, regular system updates play a significant role in compliance with industry regulations and standards. Many industries, such as finance, healthcare, and government, have strict requirements regarding the security and integrity of their IT systems. These regulations often mandate that systems be regularly updated to mitigate security risks and protect sensitive data. Failing to comply with these standards can result in hefty fines, legal consequences, or damage to an organization's reputation. By regularly applying system updates, organizations can ensure they remain compliant with relevant laws and regulations, thus avoiding potential penalties and safeguarding their standing within the industry.

One of the most common barriers to regular system updates is the concern that updates might disrupt normal business operations. There is often a fear that applying an update could cause downtime, introduce compatibility issues, or break functionality. While these concerns are valid, modern update processes are designed to minimize disruption. Many software vendors now provide options to schedule updates during off-peak hours, ensuring that systems are not affected during critical working times. Furthermore, updates are often designed to be incremental and tested to minimize the risk of introducing bugs or issues. When managed properly, regular updates can be applied with minimal impact on business continuity, and the benefits far outweigh the risks.

Another issue that some organizations face is the complexity of managing updates across a large network of systems. In enterprise environments, where hundreds or even thousands of devices and applications may be in use, ensuring that each system receives the necessary updates can be a logistical challenge. However, this problem can be mitigated through the use of automated update management tools. These tools allow administrators to schedule and deploy updates across a large number of systems simultaneously, ensuring that all devices remain up to date and secure. Automation tools can also provide reports and alerts, making it easier to track the status of updates and identify any systems that require attention. By leveraging such tools, organizations can streamline the update process and significantly reduce the risk of missing critical updates.

It is important to recognize that while system updates are essential for maintaining security and performance, they are not a catch-all solution for cybersecurity. They must be part of a broader, comprehensive security strategy that includes regular vulnerability assessments, strong access controls, and user training. Updates are effective at addressing known vulnerabilities, but they cannot protect against all threats, particularly zero-day exploits or advanced persistent threats. Therefore, while updates should be applied regularly, they should be viewed as one component of a multi-layered security approach that also includes firewalls, intrusion detection systems, and encryption.

In environments where multiple devices and platforms are used, such as in mobile or hybrid workplaces, keeping systems updated becomes even more crucial. Mobile devices, cloud platforms, and virtual machines all require their own sets of updates to ensure that they remain secure and functional. In these environments, failure to update one component can lead to vulnerabilities that affect the entire network. This interconnectedness amplifies the importance of keeping all systems, whether physical or virtual, up to date.

Ultimately, regular system updates serve as a safeguard against a multitude of issues, from security breaches and performance degradation to compatibility problems and non-compliance with regulations. They ensure that systems are functioning at their optimal level, secure from known vulnerabilities, and able to interact effectively with other technologies. In today's fast-paced and increasingly digital world, neglecting to update systems regularly is a risk that organizations and individuals cannot afford to take. The importance of regular updates goes far beyond just keeping systems running; they are a critical part of maintaining a secure, efficient, and compliant IT environment.

Identifying Vulnerabilities and Risks

In the realm of cybersecurity, the process of identifying vulnerabilities and risks is fundamental to establishing a strong defense against potential threats. It is an ongoing, dynamic process that requires constant attention to the evolving nature of technology and the methods employed by cybercriminals. Vulnerabilities, in the context of information security, refer to weaknesses in a system, network, or application that can be exploited by attackers to gain unauthorized access or disrupt the normal functioning of the system. Risks, on the other hand, refer to the likelihood of a threat exploiting a vulnerability, resulting in harm to the organization or its assets. Effectively identifying vulnerabilities and risks is the first step in any cybersecurity strategy, as it provides the foundation for prioritizing resources, mitigating threats, and preventing potential damage.

The identification of vulnerabilities begins with a thorough understanding of the system architecture, the software in use, and the network environment. Every device, operating system, application, and communication channel has its own set of potential vulnerabilities that can be targeted. These vulnerabilities might be inherent in the system due to its design, outdated software, or misconfigurations, or they may arise from external factors such as changes in the threat landscape or new attack methods. Given the sheer volume and diversity of systems in most modern organizations, it can be an overwhelming task to assess each potential vulnerability individually. Nevertheless, it is crucial to conduct regular vulnerability assessments to identify weaknesses before attackers can exploit them.

A primary tool for identifying vulnerabilities is the use of automated vulnerability scanning tools. These tools scan systems and applications for known weaknesses, such as outdated software versions, open ports, insecure configurations, or missing patches. They typically reference databases of known vulnerabilities, such as the Common Vulnerabilities and Exposures (CVE) database, to identify issues in the system that may have been previously documented by security experts. While these tools are invaluable for quickly identifying vulnerabilities, they are not foolproof. Some vulnerabilities may be specific to a given system or environment, and automated tools may not catch all potential threats. Therefore, vulnerability scanning should be supplemented with manual techniques such as code reviews, penetration testing, and audits to ensure a more comprehensive assessment.

Once vulnerabilities are identified, it is essential to assess the associated risks. Risk assessment involves determining the likelihood that a particular vulnerability will be exploited and the potential impact it could have on the organization. This process requires an understanding of the organization's assets, the criticality of the systems involved, and the potential consequences of a security breach. For example, a vulnerability in an internal HR system might pose a higher risk if the system contains sensitive employee information. Conversely, a vulnerability in a less critical system, such as a non-production web server, may present a lower risk to the organization. Risk assessment is therefore not just about identifying weaknesses but also about understanding the broader context in which they exist.

To assess risk, organizations often use a combination of qualitative and quantitative methods. Qualitative risk assessments involve subjective analysis based on factors such as the skill level of potential attackers, the value of the assets at risk, and the potential for damage. Quantitative risk assessments, on the other hand, rely on data and metrics, such as the probability of an attack occurring, the financial cost of a breach, and the potential business disruption. A balanced approach that combines both qualitative and quantitative methods can provide a clearer picture of the risks associated with each vulnerability and help organizations prioritize which issues need immediate attention.

An important aspect of identifying risks is understanding the evolving nature of cyber threats. Threats can range from common attacks, such as phishing or malware, to more sophisticated and targeted attacks like advanced persistent threats (APTs). Attackers are continually developing new techniques and tools, which means that a vulnerability that may have been considered low risk in the past could become a significant threat as attackers evolve their tactics. For this reason, identifying risks is not a one-time activity but an ongoing process that requires constant monitoring and adaptation. Organizations must stay abreast of emerging threats and trends in the cybersecurity landscape to adjust their risk management strategies accordingly.

Risk identification should also account for the potential for human error. Many of the most significant security breaches occur due to mistakes made by employees, contractors, or third-party vendors. These mistakes can range from simple misconfigurations to the accidental exposure of sensitive data. Social engineering attacks, such as phishing or spear-phishing, exploit human vulnerabilities by tricking users into divulging credentials or clicking on malicious links. In this context, identifying risks also involves assessing the effectiveness of security training programs and the overall awareness of employees regarding cybersecurity best practices.

Once vulnerabilities and risks are identified, it is crucial to communicate them effectively within the organization. This is where collaboration between IT, security teams, management, and other stakeholders becomes essential. A vulnerability might be identified by the security team, but the risk associated with that vulnerability might only be fully understood by management, who can make decisions about the appropriate resources to allocate for mitigation. A clear and transparent communication strategy ensures that the necessary steps are taken to reduce risk, such as applying patches, strengthening access controls, or investing in additional security infrastructure. Effective communication also helps to ensure that all relevant parties understand the importance of addressing identified risks in a timely manner.

The final stage in identifying vulnerabilities and risks is developing and implementing a risk mitigation strategy. Risk mitigation involves taking steps to reduce the likelihood of an attack exploiting a vulnerability or to minimize the impact if such an attack occurs. This could include applying patches, configuring firewalls, segmenting networks, enhancing authentication processes, or deploying intrusion detection systems. However, risk mitigation is not a one-size-fits-all approach. Each vulnerability and risk must be assessed on a case-by-case basis to determine the most appropriate response.

The process of identifying vulnerabilities and risks is never truly finished. As new technologies are implemented, systems are updated, and the threat landscape evolves, vulnerabilities and risks must be reassessed regularly. This continual process of evaluation, prioritization, and mitigation ensures that organizations can respond effectively to new threats and maintain a strong cybersecurity posture. The ability to identify vulnerabilities and assess the risks they pose is a critical skill for any organization striving to protect its digital assets, and it forms the cornerstone of an effective cybersecurity strategy.

The Evolution of Patch Management Practices

Patch management has evolved significantly over the years, responding to the increasing complexity of technology, the growing sophistication of cyber threats, and the rising demands for operational efficiency. From its early days as a simple process of updating software to address bugs and enhance performance, patch management has become a critical component of an organization's overall cybersecurity strategy. Today, it involves a comprehensive approach to maintaining the security and stability of systems, applications, and networks. The evolution of patch management practices mirrors the rapid advancements in IT infrastructure, the expansion of the internet, and the increasing reliance on digital systems for business operations.

In the early stages of computing, patch management was a relatively straightforward process. Software updates were often released in response to user feedback about bugs or system failures, and these updates were usually deployed manually. A system administrator would typically download patches from a vendor's website or distribution service, then apply them to individual systems. This method was feasible in the early days when computing environments were smaller, and systems were relatively simple. The scope of vulnerabilities was more limited, and the internet was not yet a primary vector for distributing malicious software or exploits. As a result, the process of patch management was largely reactive and not integrated into a broader security strategy.

As the use of computers and the internet grew, so did the complexity of software and the potential risks posed by vulnerabilities. During the 1990s and early 2000s, organizations began to realize the importance of keeping their systems updated to prevent attacks. The rapid expansion of the internet created a new vector for cyber threats, and it became clear that software vulnerabilities could be exploited by hackers to gain unauthorized access to systems, steal sensitive data, or disrupt business operations. The need for more proactive patch management practices emerged. No longer could organizations afford to wait for issues to arise before applying fixes; they had to anticipate vulnerabilities and take steps to mitigate them before they could be exploited.

At this point, patch management started to shift from a reactive task to a more proactive and systematic approach. Organizations began to implement regular patching schedules, with updates being applied to systems on a more consistent basis. This change was driven by the recognition that many attacks targeted known vulnerabilities that had already been patched by vendors, but organizations had failed to apply those patches in a timely manner. The patching process became more formalized, with guidelines and procedures being developed to ensure that patches were deployed across all systems and devices. However, even with regular updates, many organizations still struggled to keep up with the sheer volume of patches released by vendors, and the process remained cumbersome.

As systems and software became more complex, patch management practices had to adapt. The emergence of enterprise-level IT environments, where hundreds or even thousands of devices were connected to a single network, made it increasingly difficult to manually apply patches to each system. This complexity was compounded by the fact that patches sometimes conflicted with existing software or caused system instability, which could lead to costly downtime. In response to these challenges, automation tools were developed to streamline the patch management process. These tools allowed for the centralized management of patches, enabling administrators to schedule, deploy, and track patches across a wide range of systems from a single interface. Automated patch management systems helped reduce the manual effort required to apply patches and ensured that updates were deployed more consistently.

As cybersecurity threats became more sophisticated, patch management evolved to become an integral part of an organization's overall security posture. The rise of advanced persistent threats (APTs) and zero-day exploits highlighted the need for more proactive patch management practices. These types of attacks often exploited previously unknown vulnerabilities, which meant that organizations could no longer rely solely on patches for known vulnerabilities. To address this challenge, vulnerability scanning and risk assessment

19

tools were integrated into patch management processes. These tools allowed organizations to identify potential vulnerabilities in their systems before patches were released, enabling them to prioritize patches based on the severity of the risk they posed. This shift in focus toward risk-based patch management allowed organizations to better allocate resources and ensure that the most critical vulnerabilities were addressed first.

The growing complexity of IT environments further influenced the evolution of patch management practices. With the advent of cloud computing, mobile devices, and the Internet of Things (IoT), organizations now had to manage patches across a diverse array of platforms and devices. This diversity presented new challenges, as different operating systems, applications, and hardware configurations required different patching strategies. The rise of cloud-based services and virtualized environments also introduced new complexities, as organizations had to consider patching not just physical systems, but virtual machines and containers as well. Patch management practices had to become more flexible and adaptable to accommodate these changes. In many cases, organizations turned to third-party vendors and service providers to help manage patches across their cloud environments, ensuring that all systems remained up to date and secure.

Today, patch management is no longer viewed as a one-off task but as an ongoing, integrated process that requires constant attention. The frequency and urgency of patching have increased as the threat landscape has expanded and cybercriminals have become more aggressive. Organizations are now under pressure to patch systems as soon as a vulnerability is discovered, particularly when it comes to high-priority security patches. This has led to the development of more sophisticated patch management solutions that can automatically detect, prioritize, and deploy patches in real time. These solutions leverage machine learning and artificial intelligence to predict potential vulnerabilities and recommend patching actions based on historical data and trends.

Additionally, the importance of patch testing has become more pronounced. As the risks associated with patching have increased, organizations have had to implement more rigorous testing procedures to ensure that patches do not inadvertently introduce new issues or conflicts into their systems. Automated testing environments have been developed to test patches in controlled settings before they are deployed across production systems, helping to reduce the risk of downtime or performance degradation.

The evolution of patch management practices has also been influenced by regulatory and compliance requirements. Many industries, such as healthcare and finance, are subject to strict regulations that require organizations to maintain a certain level of security and compliance. These regulations often mandate that systems be kept up to date with the latest security patches to protect sensitive data and ensure business continuity. As a result, organizations have had to develop patch management practices that not only address security concerns but also ensure compliance with industry standards and regulations.

In summary, the evolution of patch management practices reflects the growing complexity of IT systems, the increasing sophistication of cyber threats, and the need for operational efficiency in today's digital landscape. From manual updates in the early days of computing to the sophisticated, automated systems used today, patch management has become a crucial element of an organization's overall cybersecurity strategy. As technology continues to evolve and cyber threats become more pervasive, patch management will remain a critical practice for ensuring the security and stability of digital systems and infrastructure.

Understanding the Different Types of Patches

In the context of software maintenance, patches are critical tools for fixing vulnerabilities, improving functionality, and maintaining the overall health of a system. However, not all patches are the same, and understanding the different types of patches available is essential for effective patch management. Patches can vary based on their purpose, the problems they address, and the scope of their impact. Over time, as the complexity of IT systems has grown, so has the variety of patches, each designed to address specific needs within a system or application. Understanding these differences is crucial for IT professionals and organizations to apply the right patches at the right time to maintain system stability, security, and performance.

At a basic level, patches can be classified according to the issues they are designed to resolve. The most common types of patches include security patches, bug fixes, performance patches, and feature updates. Security patches are perhaps the most well-known and are issued when a vulnerability is discovered in the system or software that could be exploited by attackers. These vulnerabilities might allow unauthorized access, data breaches, or even system crashes. Security patches are usually prioritized because of the immediate threat they pose to the system's integrity. They are developed to close security gaps, protect sensitive data, and prevent malicious activities such as hacking, malware infections, and denial-of-service attacks. Given the increasing number of cyber threats in the modern digital landscape, timely application of security patches is essential to prevent significant damage.

Bug fixes are another type of patch commonly issued by software vendors. Unlike security patches, bug fixes address non-critical issues or errors that affect the functionality of software or hardware. These bugs can manifest in various ways, such as causing software crashes, incorrect output, or malfunctioning features. Although bug fixes may not directly impact security, they are necessary for improving the overall user experience and ensuring that the system operates as intended. These patches are often released in response to user reports or internal testing, and they help organizations avoid unnecessary disruptions that could hinder productivity or cause operational inefficiencies. While not as urgent as security patches, bug fixes are still important for maintaining system reliability.

Performance patches are another class of updates designed to improve the efficiency and speed of a system. Over time, software can become sluggish or inefficient due to increasing demands on system resources, outdated code, or other factors. Performance patches address these issues by optimizing the software to use system resources more effectively, reduce processing times, and improve response times. These patches can have a noticeable impact on user experience and overall system performance, making them an essential part of regular software maintenance. Performance patches may also address issues such as memory leaks, slow data retrieval, or high CPU usage that could otherwise degrade the functionality of the system over time.

Feature updates are patches that introduce new functionalities or enhancements to existing features of software or applications. While security patches and bug fixes are often reactive, feature updates are generally proactive, providing new capabilities that enhance the software's usefulness or align it with emerging technologies. These updates can include anything from minor tweaks to major overhauls, such as adding new user interface elements, incorporating additional third-party integrations, or expanding the software's compatibility with newer hardware or software versions. Feature updates are often used by developers to ensure that their products remain competitive in the market by adding new functionalities that meet the evolving needs of users. While feature updates can improve the system's value, they must be carefully tested to ensure they do not introduce new bugs or incompatibilities.

In addition to these standard types of patches, there are specialized patches that address specific needs or issues within particular contexts. For example, critical updates are patches that address vulnerabilities or issues of high importance. These patches are typically released as a result of a serious threat or widespread exploit, and they are intended to be applied as quickly as possible. Critical updates may include fixes for zero-day vulnerabilities, which are security flaws that have not yet been publicly disclosed, making them particularly dangerous until patched. These updates often have a higher priority than regular security patches and are essential for preventing large-scale attacks.

Another specialized patch is a hotfix, which is typically issued outside the regular patching cycle to address urgent issues that require immediate attention. Hotfixes are often used to resolve critical system failures or to patch vulnerabilities that are being actively exploited. Unlike regular patches, hotfixes may not go through the usual testing process and might be applied directly to production systems. While hotfixes can be necessary for mitigating serious issues, they also come with a higher risk of unintended consequences, as they might not have been thoroughly tested in all environments.

Service packs are large cumulative updates that bundle together several patches, including security fixes, bug fixes, performance improvements, and new features. Service packs are typically released for major software products, such as operating systems or office suites, and represent a significant update that addresses multiple issues in one go. While service packs may contain both patches and new features, they are often released after a considerable amount of time, allowing developers to accumulate a range of fixes and improvements. Service packs are an efficient way of deploying multiple patches at once and are often seen as an essential part of maintaining older software versions, ensuring that they remain functional and secure over time.

The rise of cloud computing and mobile devices has also led to the development of cloud-specific patches and mobile updates. Cloud platforms and services require specialized patching strategies due to the distributed nature of cloud environments and the shared responsibility model between cloud providers and customers. Cloud-specific patches may address issues related to virtualization, multi-tenancy, or cloud security, and they need to be applied promptly to maintain the integrity and security of cloud-based services. Similarly, mobile devices often require unique patches that are tailored to their operating systems, such as Android or iOS. Mobile updates may address security vulnerabilities, app performance, or new features and are typically pushed out automatically to end-users.

As the variety of patches has increased, organizations have had to develop more sophisticated patch management strategies to handle the growing complexity of software environments. Automated patch management tools have become indispensable for ensuring that patches are applied efficiently and consistently across systems. These tools can automatically detect, prioritize, and deploy patches based on the severity of the issues they address, minimizing the risk of human error and reducing downtime caused by manual patching processes. With the increasing frequency of patch releases and the growing number of systems that need to be patched, these automated tools are essential for maintaining system security and performance.

The understanding of different types of patches is essential for managing software systems effectively. Each patch type serves a distinct purpose, from enhancing security to improving performance or introducing new features. As organizations continue to rely on complex IT systems, the need to apply the appropriate patches in a timely and efficient manner has become more critical than ever. A comprehensive patch management strategy that accounts for all these different types of patches ensures that systems remain secure, functional, and up to date with the latest technological advancements.

Patch Management Models: Centralized vs. Decentralized

Patch management is a critical component of any organization's cybersecurity strategy. As organizations grow in size and complexity, the need for efficient patch management practices becomes even more essential. One of the key decisions organizations must make in managing patches is whether to adopt a centralized or decentralized model. Each model offers distinct advantages and challenges, and the choice between them depends on a variety of factors, including the organization's size, structure, resources, and the complexity of its IT infrastructure. Understanding the differences between centralized and decentralized patch management models is crucial for determining which approach best suits an organization's needs and ensures optimal security and operational efficiency.

In a centralized patch management model, all patching activities are controlled and managed from a single point of authority, typically by a dedicated IT team or a centralized IT department. This approach allows for streamlined processes and ensures that all systems within the organization are kept up to date with the latest patches. The key advantage of a centralized system is the ability to maintain a consistent and coordinated approach across the entire organization. Since all patches are managed from one central location, administrators can ensure that updates are applied in a timely manner to all systems, reducing the risk of leaving any systems vulnerable to known security threats. Centralized patch management also allows for easier tracking and monitoring of patch statuses, as administrators can see in real time which systems have been updated and which still require attention.

Centralized patch management can also simplify compliance efforts. Many industries have strict regulatory requirements regarding system security and data protection, and a centralized approach can help ensure that these requirements are met consistently across the organization. By managing patches centrally, organizations can create standardized procedures for patch testing, deployment, and documentation. This uniformity helps ensure that patches are applied in accordance with industry standards and that the necessary records are maintained for compliance audits. Additionally, centralized patch management allows for better resource allocation. IT teams can focus their efforts on managing a smaller set of tasks and tools, which can lead to increased efficiency and reduced administrative overhead.

However, while centralized patch management offers several benefits, it also comes with some drawbacks. One of the primary challenges is scalability. As organizations grow in size and expand their IT infrastructure, managing patches from a central point can become increasingly difficult. In large organizations, especially those with multiple geographic locations or diverse network environments, it can be challenging to apply patches uniformly across all systems. Additionally, the centralized model may become a bottleneck in situations where a large number of patches need to be deployed at once. Delays in the central patching process can lead to missed updates and potential security vulnerabilities, particularly if the IT team is already stretched thin with other tasks. Furthermore, centralized patch management may require significant investments in infrastructure, such as patch management tools or systems that can handle the scale of large, complex environments.

In contrast, a decentralized patch management model allows individual departments, teams, or business units within the organization to manage their own patching activities. In this model, responsibility for applying patches is distributed across different areas of the organization, with each unit managing its own systems and updates. This approach offers greater flexibility, as it allows individual teams to tailor their patch management practices to the specific needs of their systems. Decentralized patch management can be particularly beneficial in organizations that operate in diverse environments or have specialized applications that require unique patching processes. For example, a research and development department may need to test patches for compatibility with proprietary software, while a sales team may require a more streamlined patching process for standard office applications. Decentralization allows these teams to address their own specific needs without waiting for central approval or coordination.

Another advantage of decentralized patch management is the ability to respond more quickly to patching needs. In centralized systems, patches must often go through a formal process of approval and testing before they are deployed across the organization. This can create delays in applying critical updates, especially in situations where patches need to be applied urgently to address a security vulnerability. In a decentralized model, individual teams can apply patches as soon as they are available, ensuring faster responses to emerging threats. Additionally, decentralized patch management can reduce the burden on central IT teams, allowing them to focus on higher-priority tasks while individual departments handle routine patching activities.

However, the decentralized approach also presents several challenges. One of the most significant drawbacks is the lack of consistency. When patching responsibilities are distributed across different departments, there is a risk that some units may apply patches in a timely manner, while others may fall behind. This inconsistency can lead to security gaps, with some systems remaining unpatched for extended periods, potentially exposing the organization to cyber threats. Decentralized patch management can also create difficulties in tracking patch status across the entire organization. Without a central repository or system to monitor updates, it can be challenging for administrators to get an overview of which systems have been patched and which have not. This lack of visibility can make it more difficult to ensure compliance with regulatory requirements or internal security policies.

Furthermore, decentralized patch management can lead to duplication of effort. In large organizations, different departments may end up managing the same patching tasks independently, which can result in inefficiencies and redundant work. This fragmentation can also lead to confusion over roles and responsibilities, as each department may have different procedures for testing, deploying, and documenting patches. The lack of coordination between teams can also lead to issues with patch compatibility, as different units may apply patches at different times or in different ways, potentially causing conflicts or system instability.

In practice, many organizations adopt a hybrid approach to patch management, combining elements of both centralized and decentralized models. In such a hybrid model, the central IT team retains overall responsibility for managing security patches and ensuring compliance with regulatory standards, while individual departments are given the flexibility to manage patches for non-critical systems or specialized applications. This approach allows organizations to balance the benefits of centralized oversight with the flexibility and responsiveness offered by decentralized patch management. Hybrid models can also help organizations scale their patching processes more effectively, as they allow the central team to focus on high-priority tasks while enabling decentralized teams to address their own patching needs.

Ultimately, the choice between a centralized or decentralized patch management model depends on the specific needs and circumstances of the organization. A centralized model is often best suited for organizations that require tight control over their IT systems and want to ensure consistency across all systems. Decentralized models, on the other hand, are ideal for organizations with diverse or specialized systems that need greater flexibility and faster patch deployment. Regardless of the model chosen, the goal should always be to ensure that patches are applied in a timely and efficient manner, minimizing security risks and maintaining system integrity. By understanding the strengths and weaknesses of each approach, organizations can develop a patch management strategy that aligns with their operational requirements and security objectives.

The Role of Automated Systems in Patch Management

The increasing complexity of modern IT environments has made patch management a critical, yet challenging, task for organizations. As technology continues to evolve, the number of software applications, operating systems, and devices that need to be maintained and updated grows exponentially. This complexity, coupled with the rising frequency and sophistication of cyber threats, has highlighted the need for efficient, scalable patch management practices. In response to these challenges, automated systems have become an essential tool for organizations aiming to streamline their patch management processes. The role of automated systems in patch management cannot be overstated, as they enable organizations to apply patches quickly and efficiently, reducing the risk of security vulnerabilities and ensuring that systems remain up to date.

Automated patch management systems are designed to handle the entire patching process, from identifying the patches required for each system to deploying them across an organization's infrastructure. These systems are particularly beneficial in large-scale IT environments where managing patches manually would be time-consuming, prone to errors, and potentially ineffective. Automated tools offer a wide range of features, including automatic detection of missing patches, scheduling of patch deployments, and tracking of patch status across multiple systems. By automating these tasks, organizations can ensure that their systems are consistently updated, minimizing the risk of leaving vulnerabilities unaddressed.

One of the primary benefits of automated patch management is its ability to streamline the identification and deployment of patches. In a traditional manual patch management process, IT administrators must individually track patches, verify their relevance, and manually apply them to systems. This process can be particularly cumbersome in environments with numerous systems and applications, where patch requirements vary between devices. Automated systems eliminate this complexity by scanning systems to identify missing patches, prioritizing them based on their severity, and applying them without manual intervention. This automated approach not only saves time but also ensures that patches are applied more consistently and without human error. For organizations with a large number of devices, automation is essential to maintain a comprehensive patch management strategy.

Another critical advantage of automated patch management is the speed with which patches can be deployed. Cyber threats, particularly those exploiting known vulnerabilities, evolve quickly. In many cases, software vendors release patches in response to newly discovered security flaws or vulnerabilities that have been actively exploited. The faster a patch can be applied, the less time an attacker has to exploit the weakness. Automated systems enable patches to be deployed as soon as they are available, without the need for manual intervention or approval processes that could delay deployment. Automated tools can also schedule patch deployments during off-hours to minimize disruptions to business operations. This rapid response is crucial in today's environment, where even a brief window of vulnerability can result in significant damage to an organization's systems and data.

Automated patch management also enhances consistency across an organization's IT infrastructure. In environments where patching is done manually, there is always the risk that certain systems may be overlooked or that patches may be applied inconsistently. Automated systems ensure that all relevant systems receive the necessary patches, regardless of their location or configuration. This consistency is especially important in organizations with diverse IT environments, where different departments may use different software or hardware configurations. By automating the process, organizations can ensure that patches are applied uniformly, reducing the likelihood of vulnerabilities remaining unpatched on certain devices or systems.

In addition to improving speed and consistency, automated systems offer better tracking and reporting capabilities. One of the challenges of manual patch management is the difficulty in keeping track of which patches have been applied, which ones are pending, and which systems require updates. Automated patch management tools provide centralized dashboards and reports that allow IT administrators to monitor the status of patch deployments in real time. These tools can also generate detailed reports that document which patches have been applied, when they were deployed, and which systems still require updates. This level of visibility is invaluable for compliance purposes, as organizations can easily demonstrate that they are adhering to industry regulations that mandate regular patching of systems.

The role of automated systems in patch management also extends to reducing downtime and minimizing disruptions. In traditional patching processes, administrators often need to manually reboot systems after applying patches, which can result in downtime and lost productivity. Automated systems can manage this process more effectively by scheduling patch deployments during non-peak hours and handling reboots automatically. Many automated systems also have built-in rollback features, which allow patches to be undone if they cause issues or conflicts with other software. This reduces the risk of operational disruptions caused by patching and ensures that systems remain stable after updates are applied.

Moreover, automated patch management systems help prioritize patches based on their criticality and potential impact. Not all patches are created equal, and some vulnerabilities present a greater risk to an organization than others. Automated systems can evaluate the severity of each patch, prioritize critical security patches, and deploy them first, ensuring that the most important updates are applied without delay. This risk-based approach ensures that patches are applied in the right order, allowing organizations to address the most pressing vulnerabilities before less critical updates.

The integration of automated patch management systems with other IT security tools further strengthens an organization's cybersecurity posture. Many automated patch management systems are designed to integrate with vulnerability scanning tools, allowing organizations to identify missing patches and vulnerabilities simultaneously. This integration enables a more holistic approach to cybersecurity, where patch management is part of a broader vulnerability management strategy. By continuously scanning systems for both missing patches and security flaws, organizations can stay ahead of emerging threats and address potential risks before they are exploited.

Despite the clear benefits, automated patch management systems are not without their challenges. One of the primary concerns is the potential for system conflicts or incompatibilities. Automated tools are designed to deploy patches across a wide range of systems, but there is always the risk that a patch may cause unintended consequences, such as breaking compatibility with other software or systems. To mitigate this risk, many organizations perform patch testing in controlled environments before deploying patches across their entire infrastructure. Automated systems can also be configured to roll back patches if they cause issues, reducing the potential for operational disruptions.

Another challenge is the complexity of managing patches in hybrid environments that include on-premises systems, cloud services, and mobile devices. Automated patch management systems must be capable of handling updates across a wide range of platforms and environments. This requires careful configuration and management to ensure that patches are applied correctly across all systems. Organizations must also ensure that they have the necessary tools and expertise to manage the security of mobile and cloud-based systems, which may have different patching requirements than traditional on-premises systems.

In large, complex organizations, automated patch management systems play a crucial role in maintaining system security and stability. The ability to quickly identify and apply patches, track patching status, and prioritize security updates ensures that systems remain up to date and protected from known vulnerabilities. By automating the patching process, organizations can reduce the risk of human error, minimize downtime, and ensure compliance with regulatory requirements. The role of automated systems in patch management will continue to grow as organizations face increasingly complex IT environments and evolving cybersecurity threats.

Patch Testing and Validation Procedures

In the world of IT security and system maintenance, patching is an essential practice to keep systems secure, functional, and up to date. While applying patches is an important step, ensuring that patches do not cause unintended side effects is equally vital. Patch testing and validation are critical processes within patch management that ensure patches are not only effective at addressing vulnerabilities but also compatible with existing systems and applications. These procedures help prevent disruptions to operations, safeguard system integrity, and ensure that patches do not inadvertently introduce new issues or conflicts. The importance of thorough testing and validation has grown as systems become more complex, and organizations increasingly rely on automated patching processes.

Patch testing refers to the process of assessing patches in a controlled environment before they are deployed across live systems. The goal of patch testing is to identify potential problems with patches, such as conflicts with existing software, hardware incompatibility, or system performance issues. Without patch testing, organizations risk deploying patches that could cause system crashes, data corruption, or application failures. Testing patches is especially important in large organizations with diverse IT environments, where different departments may be running different versions of software or hardware configurations. A patch that works in one environment may not necessarily be suitable for others, and testing helps ensure compatibility across the organization.

Patch testing generally begins with the evaluation of the patch itself. Before testing a patch, IT administrators must ensure that it addresses the intended issue, whether it is a security vulnerability, performance improvement, or bug fix. Sometimes, patches are released in response to critical security flaws, and it is vital to understand the nature of the vulnerability the patch aims to fix. This information can often be found in the vendor's patch notes or security advisory. Once the patch has been reviewed, it is deployed in a test environment that mirrors the production environment as closely as possible. This test environment is essential for evaluating the patch without risking the stability of live systems.

A key part of patch testing involves testing the functionality of the patched systems. This can include checking that the vulnerability has been addressed, that the system operates as expected, and that the patch has not introduced any new issues. Functional testing might involve running specific tests or use cases to verify that applications, services, and networks are working correctly after the patch is applied. This is particularly important for patches that address security vulnerabilities, as they must not only close the security gap but also preserve the overall functionality of the system.

Another essential aspect of patch testing is regression testing. When a patch is applied, it may affect other parts of the system that were not the intended target of the patch. Regression testing involves running tests on previously working system functionalities to ensure that they still operate correctly after the patch is applied. For instance, a patch designed to fix a vulnerability in a web server may inadvertently affect the server's ability to process user requests or handle traffic. Regression testing helps to identify such issues early in the process and allows administrators to make necessary adjustments before the patch is rolled out to the entire network.

Compatibility testing is another critical part of the patch validation process. Different systems, applications, and environments can have varying requirements, and a patch that works for one configuration may not work for another. Compatibility testing ensures that the patch does not cause conflicts with other software or hardware components. This is especially important in heterogeneous environments where various operating systems, applications, and devices must work together seamlessly. For example, a patch applied to a server might cause compatibility issues with an older version of a client application or a specific piece of network hardware. Ensuring compatibility across all system components is essential to maintaining overall system integrity.

Once a patch has passed functionality, regression, and compatibility testing in the test environment, it moves to the validation phase. Patch validation is the process of verifying that the patch achieves the desired effect without causing unintended problems. Validation typically involves monitoring the system for a period after the patch has been applied in the test environment, checking for performance issues, security vulnerabilities, or other anomalies that may have been introduced. This monitoring can include both manual observation and automated alerts to detect any deviations from normal system behavior. If any issues are identified during this phase, the patch may need to be adjusted, reissued by the vendor, or applied differently across the system.

After successful patch validation in a test environment, the patch is ready for deployment in the production environment. However, testing and validation do not end here. Continuous monitoring should be performed on the production systems after the patch is deployed to ensure that no unforeseen issues arise. This is particularly crucial for critical patches that address high-risk vulnerabilities, as even minor disruptions could have significant consequences on system operations and security. The monitoring process helps ensure that the patch is truly effective and does not introduce new vulnerabilities or performance problems in the live environment.

Automating patch testing and validation procedures has become increasingly important as organizations scale their IT environments. With the growing complexity of systems and the rapid pace at which patches are released, it is no longer feasible to rely solely on manual testing. Automated testing tools can simulate a variety of system configurations and conditions, allowing for quicker and more comprehensive testing. These tools can also provide real-time feedback, making it easier to identify issues and track patch effectiveness. Automated systems can run tests continuously, even during off-hours, ensuring that patches are tested and validated as quickly as possible while minimizing disruptions to business operations.

Despite the advantages of automation, human oversight is still necessary to ensure that testing and validation are thorough and that the correct patches are applied to the right systems. Automated systems can flag potential issues, but experienced IT administrators must analyze the results and make decisions about how to proceed. In addition, manual testing may still be required for particularly complex patches or systems that cannot be easily replicated in an automated environment.

The role of patch testing and validation is not just about preventing technical issues but also about managing risks. By testing patches before they are deployed, organizations can ensure that they are taking a proactive approach to security and system stability. Testing helps prevent costly disruptions, reduces the risk of data breaches or system failures, and ultimately contributes to a more resilient IT infrastructure. With the increasing reliance on digital systems in every aspect of business, the importance of robust patch testing and validation procedures has never been greater. Properly tested and validated patches help organizations stay ahead of emerging threats and maintain the integrity of their systems and data.

Managing Patches in Large-Scale Enterprises

In large-scale enterprises, patch management becomes a highly complex and critical task due to the sheer size and diversity of the IT infrastructure. These organizations often operate with thousands of systems spread across multiple locations, different departments, and varying network environments. Managing patches efficiently and effectively in such environments requires a well-defined strategy, robust tools, and continuous monitoring to ensure that systems remain secure, compliant, and functional. The stakes are high, as failures in patching can lead to significant vulnerabilities, data breaches, or operational disruptions. Proper patch management in large enterprises is not only about applying patches in a timely manner but also about ensuring consistency, minimizing disruption, and addressing the challenges posed by the dynamic nature of modern IT environments.

The first challenge in managing patches in large-scale enterprises is the complexity of the IT environment itself. Enterprises typically have a diverse set of systems, applications, operating systems, and devices that all require different patching strategies. Some systems may be running legacy software that needs specific updates, while others may be newer, with frequent updates from vendors. Additionally, an organization may have a mix of on-premises infrastructure, cloud environments, and mobile devices, each of which has its own set of patching requirements. This diversity can make it difficult to apply a one-size-fits-all approach to patch management. Each system or environment needs to be assessed individually, and the patching strategy must be tailored to the specific needs and vulnerabilities of the respective system.

Centralized patch management solutions are often employed by large enterprises to streamline the process. These tools enable IT teams to manage and deploy patches from a central point, reducing the complexity of patching across multiple systems and environments. A centralized system can automate the process of identifying missing patches, prioritizing them based on severity, and deploying them across the enterprise network. This level of automation significantly reduces the manual effort required to manage patches, ensuring that updates are applied consistently and in a timely manner. By centralizing the patching process, enterprises can also gain greater visibility into their patch status, making it easier to track compliance and monitor any potential vulnerabilities that remain unaddressed.

However, the use of centralized patch management solutions also comes with its own set of challenges. One of the most significant challenges is scalability. As the enterprise grows, so does the number of systems that require patching. This growth can strain centralized patch management systems, particularly when patching needs to be done across multiple geographic locations or network segments. In such cases, a single patching solution may not be able to handle the load effectively. To address this issue, enterprises often implement a distributed patch management strategy, where local IT teams in different regions or departments handle patching tasks for their specific systems, but still report back to a central authority. This hybrid approach allows for better scalability and flexibility while maintaining centralized control and oversight.

Another challenge in managing patches at scale is ensuring that all patches are thoroughly tested before deployment. Large enterprises often run mission-critical applications or systems that cannot afford to experience downtime or disruptions due to patch failures. A patch that works on one system may not work on another, especially when different systems are running varying software versions or hardware configurations. To mitigate this risk, patch testing must be conducted in controlled environments that replicate production systems as closely as possible. Testing patches in such environments allows IT teams to identify any potential issues or conflicts before they affect the live environment. This process also helps to identify which patches should be prioritized, ensuring that critical security patches are deployed first, followed by less urgent updates.

In addition to testing patches, large enterprises must also ensure that patches are deployed in a way that minimizes disruption to business operations. Patching systems during peak business hours can result in downtime, lost productivity, and frustrated users. To address this, enterprises often schedule patch deployments during off-hours or implement rolling updates, where patches are deployed in stages to avoid overwhelming the system. In some cases, enterprises may also use patching windows, where specific time slots are designated for patching activities. Automated patch management systems can help schedule these updates and monitor their progress, ensuring that patches are applied without disrupting business-critical systems.

Compliance is another crucial consideration when managing patches in large enterprises. Many industries, such as finance, healthcare, and government, are subject to stringent regulatory requirements that mandate timely patching to protect sensitive data and maintain the security of IT systems. Large enterprises must have processes in place to ensure that patches are applied in accordance with these regulations. Patch management solutions can generate detailed reports that track patch deployment and provide audit trails for compliance purposes. By maintaining these records, enterprises can demonstrate their commitment to cybersecurity and data protection, helping to avoid potential fines or legal repercussions for non-compliance.

Security patches, in particular, are of utmost importance in large-scale enterprises, as cyberattacks often target known vulnerabilities in software and systems. Unpatched systems are prime targets for attackers, who can exploit vulnerabilities to gain unauthorized access to systems, steal sensitive information, or launch more sophisticated attacks, such as ransomware. Therefore, patching must be prioritized based on the severity of the vulnerabilities being addressed. In large enterprises, a risk-based approach is often adopted, where patches that address high-risk vulnerabilities are applied first. This approach ensures that the most critical security gaps are closed immediately, reducing the likelihood of successful cyberattacks.

Despite the advantages of centralized patch management, some enterprises may opt for a decentralized or hybrid approach, particularly when dealing with specialized systems or departments that require unique patching practices. For instance, research and development departments or testing environments may require patches to be applied in a different manner than those used in the rest of the organization. In such cases, decentralized patch management allows for flexibility and customization while still maintaining overall control from the central IT team. Hybrid approaches enable organizations to combine the best of both worlds, leveraging automation for routine patching tasks while allowing for more tailored approaches when needed.

Managing patches in large-scale enterprises is a complex, ongoing process that requires careful planning, robust tools, and effective communication across departments. The need to keep systems secure, compliant, and up to date requires a strategic approach that integrates patching into the broader IT and security framework. By using centralized and automated patch management systems, enterprises can reduce the risk of vulnerabilities and ensure that patches are deployed in a timely and efficient manner. With the right tools and processes in place, large organizations can minimize the impact of patching activities, ensure compliance with regulations, and maintain a secure, stable IT environment.

Vulnerability Scanning Tools for Effective Patch Management

In the modern landscape of cybersecurity, patch management is an essential practice for securing systems and preventing attacks. However, patch management alone is not sufficient to ensure robust security. For an organization to effectively identify which patches are necessary, vulnerability scanning tools play a crucial role. These tools help organizations identify existing vulnerabilities in their systems before they can be exploited by malicious actors. By conducting regular vulnerability scans, organizations gain the visibility needed to prioritize patching efforts and deploy patches that mitigate critical risks. Vulnerability scanning tools provide detailed insights into the security health of an organization's infrastructure and are integral to effective patch management strategies.

Vulnerability scanning tools work by automatically scanning systems, networks, and applications for weaknesses or flaws that could potentially be exploited by attackers. These tools assess various components of an organization's IT infrastructure, from operating systems and applications to network devices and configurations. Once vulnerabilities are detected, the scanning tool generates reports that detail the issues, including their severity, potential impact, and whether patches or other remediation actions are available. This allows organizations to identify which patches should be applied first, based on the severity of the vulnerabilities they address. Vulnerability scanning tools essentially provide organizations with a roadmap of security gaps, helping prioritize patch deployment and resource allocation.

One of the primary benefits of using vulnerability scanning tools is the identification of known vulnerabilities. Most scanning tools leverage databases such as the Common Vulnerabilities and Exposures (CVE) system, which contains a comprehensive list of publicly known vulnerabilities. These tools match the configurations and software versions within an organization's systems against the CVE database to identify any vulnerabilities. Once a match is found, the tool can alert administrators to the existence of a potential security flaw, and patching can then be prioritized. By continuously scanning systems, vulnerability scanning tools ensure that any newly discovered vulnerabilities are detected and addressed in a timely manner, thereby helping to minimize the window of opportunity for attackers.

Beyond known vulnerabilities, vulnerability scanning tools can also identify misconfigurations and gaps in security best practices. Often, the root cause of vulnerabilities is not just outdated software, but also improper configurations that leave systems exposed. For example, certain system settings or network configurations may inadvertently open doors for attackers to exploit. Vulnerability scanners can flag these misconfigurations, providing valuable insights for administrators to correct the settings and further strengthen their defenses. These misconfigurations might include open ports, unnecessary services running, or weak password policies. Fixing these issues is equally as important as patching software vulnerabilities, and vulnerability scanning tools help ensure that these gaps are addressed.

Another advantage of vulnerability scanning tools is their ability to assess the effectiveness of existing security controls. Vulnerabilities are not always just technical flaws; they can also involve gaps in security measures such as firewalls, intrusion detection systems, or encryption protocols. A vulnerability scanner can simulate various attack scenarios, allowing organizations to assess how well their current security defenses are working. This is particularly important in organizations with complex, multi-layered security architectures. The findings from these assessments help administrators strengthen their security posture by making adjustments to defense mechanisms where necessary. Through periodic scans, organizations can continually evaluate their security defenses and adapt their patch management strategy accordingly.

Vulnerability scanning tools also provide invaluable support for compliance with industry regulations and standards. Many industries, such as healthcare, finance, and government, are subject to stringent security and privacy regulations that mandate regular vulnerability assessments. For example, regulations like the Health Insurance Portability and Accountability Act (HIPAA) or the Payment Card Industry Data Security Standard (PCI DSS) require organizations to regularly identify and address vulnerabilities to protect sensitive data. Vulnerability scanning tools simplify the process of demonstrating compliance by automatically generating reports that document vulnerabilities, remediation efforts, and patching status. This ensures that organizations can provide the necessary evidence during audits, avoiding costly penalties or legal issues.

For organizations with large and dynamic IT environments, vulnerability scanning tools help reduce the complexity of patch management. In large enterprises, there may be thousands of systems, applications, and devices that need to be patched. Manually tracking vulnerabilities across this vast infrastructure can be overwhelming and prone to errors. Vulnerability scanning tools automate the identification process, scanning the entire environment at once and producing actionable insights. This significantly reduces the manual effort required to find vulnerabilities, allowing IT teams to focus their time and resources on applying patches and other remediation activities. Automated vulnerability scans can be scheduled to run at regular intervals, ensuring that the organization's security remains up to date and that vulnerabilities are addressed promptly.

Another key benefit of vulnerability scanning tools is their ability to prioritize vulnerabilities based on their severity and potential impact.

Not all vulnerabilities are equal; some pose an immediate and severe risk to the organization, while others may be less critical. Vulnerability scanning tools typically assign a risk rating to each identified vulnerability, based on factors such as the ease of exploitation, the potential impact, and the availability of exploits in the wild. By prioritizing vulnerabilities based on these ratings, organizations can allocate their resources more efficiently, focusing on the most critical issues first. This approach ensures that patches for high-risk vulnerabilities are deployed as quickly as possible, minimizing the chances of an attacker exploiting a critical flaw.

Despite the many advantages of vulnerability scanning tools, organizations must be mindful of the limitations of these tools. While vulnerability scanners are excellent at detecting known vulnerabilities, they are not foolproof. For example, scanners may not always identify zero-day vulnerabilities, which are newly discovered flaws that are not yet included in vulnerability databases. Furthermore, vulnerability scanners may generate false positives, flagging vulnerabilities that are not actually present in the environment. To mitigate these issues, it is essential to pair vulnerability scanning with other security practices, such as penetration testing and threat intelligence feeds, to gain a more comprehensive understanding of the organization's security posture. Manual validation of scan results is also recommended to ensure the accuracy of findings.

Vulnerability scanning tools must also be integrated into a broader patch management strategy to be truly effective. While scanning tools can identify vulnerabilities, the process of patching systems and addressing issues requires coordination across multiple teams and departments. Vulnerability scanners provide the necessary information to prioritize patches, but the patching process itself must be efficient and thorough. Without proper patch management workflows in place, the findings from vulnerability scans could go unaddressed, leaving systems open to attacks.

Overall, vulnerability scanning tools are an integral component of an effective patch management strategy. They provide the visibility necessary to identify vulnerabilities, misconfigurations, and weaknesses in security controls. By automating the scanning process, vulnerability scanners help organizations stay ahead of potential threats, ensuring that patches are applied in a timely and organized manner. These tools are essential for identifying and addressing critical vulnerabilities, improving compliance, and reducing the risk of security breaches. With the ever-evolving nature of cyber threats, vulnerability scanning remains a cornerstone of proactive cybersecurity, making it an indispensable part of patch management in modern organizations.

The Challenges of Patch Management in Legacy Systems

As organizations continue to evolve and adopt new technologies, they are often faced with the challenge of maintaining and managing legacy systems. Legacy systems are older hardware or software that may no longer be supported by the original manufacturers or developers. While these systems may still function effectively for certain tasks, their maintenance becomes increasingly complex as time progresses. One of the most significant challenges associated with legacy systems is patch management. Unlike newer systems, which often benefit from regular updates and support from vendors, legacy systems may require specialized attention when it comes to patching. The risks associated with inadequate patch management in legacy systems are high, as these systems are often more vulnerable to security breaches, software bugs, and compatibility issues.

Legacy systems are often found in industries and organizations where stability and continuity of operations are paramount. Many organizations continue to rely on legacy systems because they are deeply integrated into business operations or handle critical functions that newer systems cannot easily replicate. For example, older mainframe systems or custom-built applications may have been in place for decades, performing specific functions that are vital to the organization's operations. However, as technology advances, these systems become increasingly difficult to manage, particularly when it comes to patch management. One of the primary challenges of patching legacy systems is the lack of vendor support. As software vendors discontinue their support for older versions of products, they stop releasing security patches, updates, and fixes. This leaves organizations with limited options for addressing vulnerabilities in the system, and failure to apply patches can expose the organization to significant risks.

The absence of vendor support also means that many legacy systems run outdated or obsolete software, which is more susceptible to vulnerabilities. Over time, as new security vulnerabilities are discovered in older software, they remain unaddressed because patches are no longer available. This increases the risk of exploitation by cybercriminals, who often target known vulnerabilities in unsupported systems. For example, older versions of operating systems such as Windows XP or legacy applications like older versions of Java are prime targets for hackers because they no longer receive updates to close these security gaps. With no patching support, organizations must find alternative solutions, such as applying third-party patches or implementing additional security measures like firewalls and intrusion detection systems. However, these workarounds are often less effective than regular vendor-issued updates, leaving organizations exposed to potential attacks.

Another challenge of patch management in legacy systems is the difficulty of applying patches to systems that are highly customized. Many legacy systems are not off-the-shelf products but are instead custom-built applications tailored to meet specific business needs. These systems often feature intricate codebases and complex dependencies that make patching a complicated task. Applying a patch to such systems may require extensive testing and validation to ensure that it does not interfere with the unique configurations or functionalities of the system. Unlike standardized software, where patches are designed to be broadly applicable, custom systems require more meticulous management. This can result in longer testing and deployment times, as well as increased risks of causing system disruptions or failures if the patch is incompatible with the existing codebase.

In addition to customizations, legacy systems often rely on outdated hardware that can further complicate the patching process. Older hardware may not support newer operating systems or software versions, limiting the options available for applying patches. In some cases, the hardware may be so old that it is no longer compatible with modern security tools or patching mechanisms. For example, a legacy system that runs on hardware with limited processing power or memory may struggle to handle the additional load of applying security patches. This can create a situation where the organization must choose between maintaining the old hardware and applying patches or upgrading to newer systems that can more easily accommodate modern security measures.

The complexity of managing patches in legacy systems is further compounded by the lack of skilled personnel who are familiar with the older technologies. Many IT professionals today are trained on current technologies and may lack the experience or expertise required to manage legacy systems effectively. As older systems continue to age, the pool of skilled professionals who are capable of maintaining them dwindles. This shortage of expertise can make patch management more difficult, as organizations may struggle to find qualified personnel to oversee the patching process. Furthermore, the knowledge of legacy systems often resides with employees who have been with the organization for years. If these employees retire or leave, organizations may be left with limited institutional knowledge about how to maintain and patch these systems.

Another significant challenge is the potential for business disruption when patches are applied to legacy systems. Many legacy systems are critical to day-to-day operations, and taking them offline for patching or maintenance can lead to significant business interruptions. For example, in industries such as banking, healthcare, or manufacturing, even a short downtime can result in lost productivity, revenue, or compliance violations. As a result, organizations must carefully plan patching activities to minimize disruption to operations. This often means scheduling patches during off-hours or on weekends, but even then, there is always the risk that applying patches could cause unforeseen issues that impact business continuity. The complexity of legacy systems means that patches may have unexpected side effects, such as causing system crashes, application failures, or data corruption. Without proper testing and validation, organizations run the risk of introducing new problems when attempting to fix old ones.

In some cases, legacy systems may be too critical or deeply embedded in the organization to justify the effort of patching. When this happens, organizations may need to make a difficult decision about whether to continue supporting the legacy system or invest in replacing it with a more modern solution. This is often a costly and resource-intensive process that requires careful planning and a thorough understanding of the risks involved. Replacing a legacy system may require significant time and financial resources, as well as careful data migration, retraining of staff, and integration with existing systems. While upgrading to newer systems can resolve many of the patching challenges associated with legacy systems, it is not always a feasible option for all organizations, particularly those with limited budgets or complex, mission-critical systems that cannot be easily replaced.

One possible solution for managing legacy systems is to implement additional security measures to protect them in the absence of patches. For example, network segmentation can help isolate legacy systems from other parts of the network, reducing the risk of an attacker exploiting a vulnerability in a legacy system to gain access to more critical resources. Similarly, organizations can deploy more advanced firewalls, intrusion detection systems, and antivirus software to help mitigate the risks associated with unpatched legacy systems. However, these measures are not a substitute for patching and can only provide limited protection. Ultimately, the lack of patching support for legacy systems remains a significant risk that requires careful management and consideration.

Managing patches in legacy systems is a difficult, ongoing process that requires organizations to balance the need for security with the challenges of maintaining outdated technology. Without proper patching, legacy systems become increasingly vulnerable to cyber threats and operational disruptions. However, patching legacy systems is often more complicated and resource-intensive than patching newer systems, as it involves dealing with outdated software, hardware incompatibilities, custom configurations, and a shortage of skilled personnel. To mitigate these challenges, organizations must develop strategic patch management practices that account for the unique requirements of legacy systems while minimizing the risks they pose to security and business continuity.

Understanding the Patch Lifecycle

The patch lifecycle is a critical process within the realm of IT management, particularly when it comes to maintaining secure, stable, and efficient systems. Patches are essential updates that address security vulnerabilities, improve system performance, and fix bugs. However, understanding the entire lifecycle of a patch—from its creation to its deployment and post-implementation monitoring—is vital for ensuring that patches are applied in a timely and effective manner. The patch lifecycle involves several stages, each of which plays an important role in maintaining system integrity and reducing the risk of exploitation due to unpatched vulnerabilities. These stages include identification, testing, deployment, verification, and post-deployment support.

The first stage of the patch lifecycle is identification, which involves the discovery of the issue that requires patching. This stage begins when a vulnerability or flaw is identified in the system, whether by the software vendor, a security researcher, or even an internal team. The vulnerability could be discovered through various means, such as routine testing, vulnerability scans, or external reports. Once a vulnerability is identified, the vendor or software provider typically assesses the risk and determines whether a patch is necessary. This can take time, as the vendor must analyze the problem, develop a solution, and verify that the patch will resolve the issue without introducing new problems. During this phase, it is essential that organizations remain vigilant by regularly monitoring updates from their vendors and security advisories to stay informed of potential vulnerabilities that may require attention.

Once the patch has been identified and created, the next stage is patch development. The development phase is where the patch is written, tested, and refined. The vendor's development team works to create a patch that effectively addresses the identified vulnerability while ensuring that it does not disrupt the functionality of the system or cause compatibility issues. This stage can vary in duration, depending on the severity of the vulnerability and the complexity of the system involved. For critical vulnerabilities, patches are typically developed quickly and released as emergency updates, whereas less urgent patches may take longer to develop. It is also during this phase that the patch is documented, with details about what the patch addresses, any known issues, and specific instructions for installation. Proper documentation is essential for IT administrators, as it helps them understand the scope of the patch and any potential risks or impacts.

Once the patch has been developed, it enters the testing phase. Testing is crucial to ensure that the patch works as intended and does not create additional problems or conflicts within the system. During this phase, the patch is deployed in a controlled test environment that simulates the actual production system. The goal of testing is to identify any unintended consequences or bugs that may arise when the patch is applied to the system. This process may involve regression testing to ensure that the patch does not interfere with existing functionality, as well as compatibility testing to check if the patch is compatible with different software versions or configurations. In some cases, testing also includes performance assessments to determine whether the patch affects the system's efficiency or stability. If any issues are found during testing, the patch may need to be revised and retested before it is considered ready for deployment. Successful testing ensures that the patch will not disrupt business operations or introduce new vulnerabilities.

After a patch passes testing, it moves into the deployment phase. This is the stage where the patch is applied to the production environment, and it is typically when most of the logistical challenges arise. Deployment must be carefully managed to minimize disruptions to business operations, particularly in large-scale environments where downtime can have significant consequences. In many cases, patches are deployed in a staged manner, where they are first applied to a small group of systems or departments to ensure they do not cause issues before being rolled out across the entire network. Some organizations use patch management tools to automate the deployment process, making it faster and more consistent. However, automation does not eliminate the need for careful planning and oversight, as even well-tested patches can occasionally cause unexpected issues in the live environment. During deployment, IT teams must monitor the process closely to address any potential problems quickly.

Once the patch has been deployed, it enters the verification stage. Verification is the process of confirming that the patch has been successfully applied and that it has resolved the intended issue. IT administrators must ensure that the vulnerability has been addressed and that the patch has not caused any new problems or regressions in the system. Verification typically involves running diagnostic tests, monitoring system performance, and gathering feedback from users to ensure that everything is functioning as expected. This stage is critical for ensuring that the patch does not create further disruptions or issues that could affect business operations. If any problems arise during verification, the patch may need to be rolled back, or additional fixes may be required to resolve the new issues. Additionally, verification helps to confirm that the patch has achieved its intended security outcomes, ensuring that the system is protected from exploitation by attackers.

The final stage of the patch lifecycle is post-deployment support. Even after a patch has been successfully applied and verified, ongoing monitoring and support are necessary to ensure that it continues to function as expected. Post-deployment support may involve periodic audits or scans to ensure that the system remains secure and that no new vulnerabilities have emerged. This stage also involves tracking the long-term effectiveness of the patch and addressing any user-reported issues or bugs that may not have been detected during initial testing. As new vulnerabilities are discovered or new threats emerge, patches may need to be updated or replaced, and the lifecycle begins again. In addition to monitoring the effectiveness of the patch, post-deployment support may include educating users about the changes introduced by the patch and ensuring they are aware of any new functionality or security measures.

Throughout the entire patch lifecycle, communication plays a critical role in ensuring that the patching process is efficient and effective. IT administrators, developers, and vendors must work closely together to ensure that patches are identified, tested, deployed, and verified successfully. Effective communication with end-users is also essential to ensure that they are aware of any changes to the system and to gather feedback on any issues that arise after deployment. Regular monitoring and proactive management of patches help to ensure that the organization's systems remain secure, compliant, and functional.

The patch lifecycle is a complex and ongoing process that requires careful coordination, testing, and monitoring. Each stage of the lifecycle—from identification and development to deployment, verification, and post-deployment support—plays a crucial role in maintaining the security and stability of systems. By understanding the patch lifecycle and following best practices at each stage, organizations can minimize vulnerabilities, improve system performance, and reduce the risk of security breaches. Effective patch management is a vital part of an organization's overall cybersecurity strategy, and a well-executed patch lifecycle ensures that systems remain secure, functional, and resilient in the face of evolving threats.

Developing a Comprehensive Patch Management Policy

A comprehensive patch management policy is an essential framework for ensuring that an organization's systems, applications, and infrastructure remain secure, stable, and compliant with relevant regulations. Given the increasing sophistication of cyber threats and the constant need for systems to stay up to date with the latest security updates, having a structured approach to patch management is more crucial than ever. A well-developed patch management policy defines the guidelines, responsibilities, and processes needed to ensure that patches are applied consistently and efficiently across the organization. It provides the foundation for addressing vulnerabilities, minimizing downtime, and protecting the integrity of IT systems and data.

The first step in developing a comprehensive patch management policy is to clearly define the scope of the policy. This involves identifying which systems, applications, and devices will be covered by the policy. Depending on the size and complexity of the organization, the scope may include everything from servers, workstations, and network devices to mobile devices, cloud environments, and third-party applications. It is essential to consider all possible assets that could be exposed to security risks and include them in the patch management process. The policy should also specify the frequency of patching for each type of system. While critical systems may need immediate patching whenever a vulnerability is discovered, other less critical systems might only need patching on a regular basis, such as once a month or quarterly. Defining these parameters at the outset ensures that there is a clear understanding of what needs to be patched and how frequently.

Once the scope is defined, the next step is to establish a process for identifying patches and vulnerabilities. This involves setting up mechanisms for monitoring security advisories, vendor updates, and vulnerability databases. It is essential to stay informed of the latest patches released by software vendors, as well as new vulnerabilities that could pose a risk to the organization's systems. This process may include subscribing to relevant threat intelligence feeds, vulnerability databases like the Common Vulnerabilities and Exposures (CVE) system, and security bulletins from trusted sources. In larger organizations, automated tools can be used to scan systems for missing patches and identify vulnerabilities that need to be addressed. By implementing regular scanning, organizations can proactively identify issues before they become critical problems.

One of the most important aspects of a patch management policy is determining the prioritization of patches. Not all patches are created equal, and it is crucial to prioritize patches based on the severity of the vulnerabilities they address. High-priority patches should be those that address critical security flaws or vulnerabilities that are actively being exploited in the wild. These patches should be deployed as quickly as possible to mitigate the risk of a cyber-attack. Lower-priority patches, on the other hand, might address performance improvements or minor bugs that do not have an immediate impact on security. These patches can typically be scheduled for deployment during regular maintenance windows. A well-defined patch prioritization strategy ensures that resources are allocated effectively, and the most critical patches are addressed first.

After determining patch priorities, the policy should specify the testing procedures for patches. Testing is an essential step in the patch management process, as it ensures that patches will not cause system instability, break existing functionality, or introduce new vulnerabilities. Patches should first be applied in a controlled testing environment that replicates the production environment as closely as possible. This environment should include various systems, applications, and configurations to test the patch across different use cases. During testing, it is important to evaluate the patch for its impact on system performance, compatibility with other software, and overall stability. Only once the patch has passed testing and verification should it be deployed in the live environment. Defining the testing procedures within the policy ensures that patches are rigorously assessed and that potential issues are identified before they affect the organization's operations.

Another critical aspect of the patch management policy is deployment. The policy should outline the procedures for rolling out patches across the organization's IT infrastructure. It is essential to ensure that patches are deployed in a controlled and systematic manner to minimize downtime and operational disruption. Patching should, whenever possible, be done during off-peak hours or scheduled maintenance windows to avoid interference with business operations. For larger organizations, deploying patches in stages may be necessary. This involves first applying patches to a small group of systems or departments and then gradually expanding deployment to the entire organization. Automated patch management tools can play a significant role in streamlining the deployment process by ensuring that patches are applied consistently across all systems and reducing the risk of human error.

The policy should also define the procedures for verifying and monitoring the effectiveness of patches once they have been deployed. Verification ensures that the patch has successfully addressed the vulnerability and that no new issues have been introduced into the system. This process may involve running diagnostic tests, performing vulnerability scans, and gathering feedback from users. Continuous monitoring is necessary to ensure that the patched systems remain secure and functional. If any issues arise post-deployment, the policy should outline the steps for troubleshooting and rolling back patches if necessary. Monitoring tools can help track the patch status across the organization, providing administrators with visibility into which systems are up to date and which still require attention.

Another important element of a patch management policy is ensuring compliance with regulatory requirements. Many industries are subject to specific regulations that mandate the timely application of security patches. For instance, the healthcare sector must comply with HIPAA, which requires organizations to protect sensitive patient data by implementing security measures, including regular patching of systems. Similarly, the financial industry is governed by the PCI DSS, which mandates patching of vulnerabilities in systems handling payment card information. The patch management policy should include guidelines for maintaining compliance with these and other relevant regulations. This may involve keeping detailed records of all patches applied, maintaining an audit trail of patching activities, and ensuring that the organization meets any required patching deadlines.

Finally, the policy should include provisions for ongoing improvement and adaptation. The landscape of cybersecurity is constantly evolving, and new vulnerabilities and threats emerge regularly. As such, a comprehensive patch management policy should be reviewed and updated periodically to address changes in the organization's IT environment, new security threats, and advancements in patch management technologies. The policy should also ensure that staff members receive regular training to stay informed about best practices in patch management and to develop the necessary skills to handle patching tasks effectively. Continuous improvement of the patch management process helps to ensure that systems remain secure and that the organization can respond to new challenges in a timely manner.

A comprehensive patch management policy is essential for maintaining the security, stability, and compliance of an organization's IT systems. By clearly defining the scope, processes, prioritization, testing, deployment, and monitoring of patches, organizations can significantly reduce the risks associated with unpatched vulnerabilities. The policy ensures that patches are applied in a systematic and efficient manner, minimizing disruption to business operations and protecting the organization from potential cyber threats.

Patch Deployment Strategies for Minimal Disruption

Patch deployment is a critical task in patch management, and it requires a strategic approach to ensure that systems are kept secure and up to date without disrupting business operations. In many organizations, patching is a necessary yet often disruptive process, particularly when critical updates need to be applied to systems that are integral to daily business functions. As organizations rely more heavily on their IT infrastructure for everything from communications and customer service to manufacturing and financial operations, minimizing the impact of patch deployments has become a priority. The right deployment strategy can help balance the need for timely patching with the need to maintain continuous, uninterrupted operations.

One of the most important strategies for minimizing disruption during patch deployment is proper planning and scheduling. For many organizations, especially those with large-scale environments, patching during peak business hours can result in slowdowns, system outages, or decreased productivity. To minimize this impact, it is crucial to schedule patch deployments during non-peak times, such as overnight or on weekends. This minimizes the risk of affecting employees' ability to work, customers' access to services, or critical business functions that rely on IT systems. Careful scheduling also ensures that the patching process is done at a time when IT staff can be available to monitor the deployment and respond quickly to any issues that arise.

Additionally, patch deployment strategies should include the use of phased or staged rollouts. Instead of deploying patches to an entire organization or system in one go, phased rollouts allow patches to be applied in smaller, controlled increments. This can be especially useful in large organizations or complex environments with diverse systems. For example, patches can first be deployed to a small group of test systems or a single department. Once the patch has been successfully applied and any potential issues have been addressed, it can then be rolled out to other systems, gradually covering the entire organization. Phased rollouts help reduce the risk of widespread disruptions if a patch causes unexpected issues, as the impact is initially contained to a smaller group of users or systems. This incremental approach allows for more careful monitoring and troubleshooting before the patch is fully deployed across the enterprise.

Automation also plays a significant role in minimizing disruption during patch deployment. Automated patch deployment tools allow for the smooth application of patches across multiple systems without requiring significant manual effort. These tools can schedule and deploy patches according to predefined parameters, ensuring that they are applied consistently and on time. Automation also helps reduce the risk of human error, which can be a source of disruption when patches are applied manually. IT teams can set up automated systems to deploy patches at optimal times, monitor the progress of deployment, and quickly address any failures or issues that occur. By using automated patch deployment tools, organizations can streamline the process, reduce the time spent on patching, and ensure that patches are applied without unnecessary delays or errors.

Another strategy for minimizing disruption during patch deployment is testing patches before deployment. Testing ensures that patches will not cause conflicts with existing software, hardware, or configurations in the production environment. In a large enterprise with diverse systems, testing is particularly important, as a patch that works well on one system may not function correctly on another. Testing should be conducted in a controlled environment that mirrors the production environment as closely as possible. This allows IT teams to identify any potential issues before deploying the patch across the organization. By running the patch in a test environment, IT staff can evaluate its impact on system performance, compatibility, and security, ensuring that it will not disrupt business operations when deployed. Additionally, conducting thorough testing helps determine whether the patch introduces new issues or fails to resolve the vulnerabilities it was designed to address.

Rollback strategies are another important consideration when developing patch deployment strategies. Despite careful planning, testing, and staging, patches may still cause issues in the live environment. If a patch causes system instability, crashes, or compatibility problems, it is essential to have a rollback procedure in place. Rollback procedures allow IT administrators to revert systems to their previous state before the patch was applied, minimizing downtime and disruption. Rollback strategies should be carefully planned and tested as part of the deployment process to ensure they work effectively when needed. In some cases, it may be necessary to use automated rollback tools that can quickly undo changes and restore systems to their previous configurations. Having a reliable rollback strategy in place provides an additional layer of protection and ensures that the impact of patch deployment failures is minimized.

Communication is also a critical element of a successful patch deployment strategy. Prior to deploying patches, it is important to communicate with end users and stakeholders about the upcoming changes. Users should be informed of when patches will be applied, what systems may be affected, and how long they can expect any downtime or disruptions to last. Clear communication helps manage expectations and reduces frustration when patch deployments do cause disruptions. In addition, communication should be ongoing during the deployment process. IT teams should provide real-time updates on the status of patch deployment and quickly address any issues that arise. Post-deployment communication is also important to notify users that the patch has been applied successfully and that any required follow-up actions have been completed.

For organizations with highly sensitive or mission-critical systems, additional precautions may be necessary. Critical systems often cannot afford any downtime, even during off-peak hours. In these cases, more advanced deployment strategies may be required. For example, systems can be patched using a redundant configuration, where backup systems are temporarily brought online to replace the primary systems while they are patched. Once the patch is successfully deployed and verified, the systems can be switched back to their original configuration. This approach ensures that there is no disruption to services, even during patching. Another strategy is to apply patches in a more granular fashion, deploying updates to individual components or services rather than the entire system at once. This reduces the likelihood of system-wide failures and allows the organization to maintain operations even during patching.

In organizations where business continuity is paramount, maintaining a detailed patch management plan is essential for minimizing disruptions. The plan should outline the steps and strategies for patch deployment, as well as the roles and responsibilities of the IT team, stakeholders, and end users. The plan should also include contingency measures, such as backup strategies, rollback procedures, and communication protocols, to ensure that patching does not negatively impact the organization's operations. By developing a comprehensive patch management plan, organizations can ensure that patch deployments are carried out with minimal disruption, while still addressing critical security vulnerabilities and maintaining system performance.

Patch deployment is an essential part of maintaining secure and efficient IT systems, but it can also be disruptive if not managed carefully. Through thoughtful planning, testing, communication, and automation, organizations can minimize the impact of patch deployments, ensuring that systems remain up to date without compromising business continuity. By adopting strategies such as phased rollouts, automated patching, and rollback procedures, organizations can manage the complexity of patch deployment in a way that maintains security and operational efficiency.

Managing Security Patches in Cloud Environments

As organizations increasingly adopt cloud services for their IT infrastructure, managing security patches in cloud environments has become a critical concern for maintaining the integrity and security of their data and systems. The shift to cloud computing has introduced both significant benefits and unique challenges, particularly when it comes to patch management. While cloud environments offer flexibility, scalability, and cost efficiency, they also present a shared responsibility model between the cloud provider and the customer. Understanding how to manage security patches in this context is essential for ensuring that vulnerabilities are addressed promptly and that systems remain secure.

In traditional on-premises environments, organizations have complete control over their IT infrastructure, including patch management. However, in cloud environments, the responsibility for managing security patches is often divided between the cloud service provider and the customer. Cloud providers are generally responsible for patching the underlying infrastructure, including the physical servers, network components, and hypervisors that support the cloud services. This is typically referred to as the "security of the cloud." On the other hand, customers are responsible for patching the software and applications they deploy on top of the cloud infrastructure, which is known as the "security in the cloud." This division of responsibility means that organizations must understand which patches are their responsibility and which fall under the purview of the cloud provider.

One of the primary challenges of managing security patches in cloud environments is maintaining visibility and control over the systems and applications that the organization is responsible for patching. In a cloud environment, resources are often dynamic and distributed across multiple regions and data centers. Instances can be spun up or down based on demand, making it difficult for organizations to keep track of all the systems that require patching. Unlike traditional on-premises environments, where servers and devices are physically controlled and monitored, cloud environments can change rapidly, making it more challenging to ensure that all systems are up to date with the latest patches. Additionally, many organizations may use multi-cloud or hybrid environments, which further complicates the patch management process as different cloud providers may have different patching schedules and requirements.

To address these challenges, organizations must implement robust patch management practices that include automated tools and centralized systems to track and manage patches across cloud resources. Automated patch management tools can help identify vulnerabilities, track missing patches, and deploy updates consistently across cloud-based instances. These tools can also be configured to perform regular scans of cloud resources to identify outdated or unpatched systems. By leveraging automation, organizations can ensure that patches are applied in a timely manner, reducing the risk of security breaches due to unpatched vulnerabilities. Furthermore, centralized patch management platforms can provide visibility into the status of patches across various cloud services and environments, enabling IT teams to maintain a comprehensive view of their patching efforts.

Another key challenge in managing security patches in cloud environments is ensuring that patches do not introduce conflicts or disruptions to the business. In cloud environments, especially those running mission-critical applications, patch deployment must be carefully planned to minimize downtime and avoid system instability. Unlike on-premises environments, where maintenance windows can be scheduled with a degree of certainty, cloud environments often require patches to be deployed across multiple instances and geographic regions. This makes it more difficult to predict the impact of patching activities on business operations. To mitigate this risk, organizations should develop a patch testing and validation process that allows them to test patches in isolated environments before they are deployed to production systems. Testing ensures that patches will not cause disruptions, application failures, or compatibility issues, particularly in complex cloud environments with interdependent services and applications.

Moreover, patching in cloud environments must take into account the unique security considerations of multi-tenant architectures. In public cloud environments, multiple customers share the same underlying infrastructure, which means that the patching process must ensure that vulnerabilities are addressed without affecting the privacy or security of other tenants. Cloud providers typically implement isolation mechanisms to ensure that customer data and workloads are separated, but customers must still be vigilant in ensuring that the applications and services they deploy are secure and properly patched. For instance, patching a shared cloud service or database platform could impact all users of that service, so cloud providers need to coordinate with customers to ensure that patches are applied without causing disruptions to other tenants. Organizations must also ensure that any third-party applications or services they use within the cloud are kept up to date with the latest security patches.

A critical aspect of patch management in cloud environments is compliance with regulatory requirements. Many industries, such as healthcare, finance, and government, are subject to strict data protection regulations that mandate regular patching of systems and applications to mitigate the risk of data breaches and security vulnerabilities. Cloud providers often offer compliance certifications that demonstrate their adherence to specific security standards and regulations. However, customers must also ensure that their own systems, applications, and services in the cloud meet these requirements. Organizations should work closely with their cloud providers to understand the security features and patching processes offered by the provider, while also taking responsibility for ensuring that their own workloads are compliant. Regular audits and assessments should be conducted to ensure that the cloud environment is up to date with the latest security patches and that any gaps in compliance are addressed promptly.

Managing patches in cloud environments also requires organizations to stay informed about new threats and vulnerabilities. Cybercriminals are constantly discovering new exploits, and patching must be done as soon as vulnerabilities are discovered and patches are made available. To stay ahead of emerging threats, organizations should subscribe to security advisories, threat intelligence feeds, and vendor notifications. Cloud providers often provide customers with security bulletins that announce critical patches and updates, but it is ultimately up to the organization to act on these alerts and apply the necessary patches in a timely manner. Establishing an efficient process for reviewing and responding to security alerts is vital for ensuring that cloud systems remain secure.

One potential solution to streamline the patching process in cloud environments is the use of containerization and microservices. By breaking applications into smaller, manageable components, organizations can isolate patches and updates to specific containers or services without affecting the entire application. This allows for more flexible and targeted patching, reducing the risk of downtime or disruptions to the broader system. Container orchestration platforms, such as Kubernetes, can also automate the patching and updating of containers, further reducing the manual effort involved in patch management. Similarly, organizations can use Infrastructure as Code (IaC) practices to automate the configuration and patching of cloud resources, ensuring that systems are always deployed with the latest security updates.

Managing security patches in cloud environments requires a proactive and systematic approach. By implementing automated tools, leveraging centralized management platforms, and maintaining a robust testing and validation process, organizations can ensure that their cloud environments remain secure and compliant. It is essential to maintain a clear understanding of the shared responsibility model, stay informed about emerging threats, and work closely with cloud providers to coordinate patch management efforts. With the right strategy in place, organizations can effectively manage patches in cloud environments, reducing the risk of vulnerabilities and ensuring that their systems remain secure, stable, and compliant with regulatory standards.

Patch Management for IoT Devices and Embedded Systems

The rapid proliferation of Internet of Things (IoT) devices and embedded systems in both consumer and industrial applications has introduced a new layer of complexity to the field of patch management. These devices, ranging from smart thermostats and wearables to industrial control systems and medical devices, are often interconnected and play a critical role in everyday operations. However, they also present unique challenges when it comes to keeping them secure. Unlike traditional computing devices, IoT devices and embedded systems often have limited resources in terms of processing power, storage, and network connectivity, which can complicate the application of security patches. Effective patch management for these devices is essential to mitigate the risks associated with vulnerabilities and to ensure the continued safe and reliable operation of these systems.

One of the primary challenges in patching IoT devices and embedded systems is the sheer diversity of these devices. There is a vast range of manufacturers, each with different architectures, operating systems, and communication protocols. This heterogeneity makes it difficult to implement a one-size-fits-all patching approach. Additionally, many IoT devices are designed with minimal computing resources, which can limit the ability to install or even support patches. In some cases, the device may not have sufficient memory or processing power to run complex security updates, forcing manufacturers to release simplified patches or update mechanisms that are often less effective than traditional updates applied to more powerful systems. The limitations of these devices can make patching challenging, as it is not always possible to install updates without disrupting the device's functionality or performance.

Another significant issue is the difficulty in updating IoT devices and embedded systems once they have been deployed. Unlike software applications on computers or smartphones, IoT devices are often installed in remote or hard-to-reach locations. Many of these devices are integrated into physical infrastructures, such as factories, homes, or medical facilities, and are often difficult to access for maintenance or updates. This means that applying patches to these devices is not as simple as remotely updating a desktop or mobile device. Some IoT devices may not have direct network access or may be installed in environments where connectivity is intermittent or unreliable. This makes it more difficult to remotely push patches and updates, leaving devices exposed to security vulnerabilities until they can be physically accessed or reconnected to a network for patching.

The extended lifespan of many IoT devices further complicates patch management. IoT devices are often designed to operate for years, sometimes decades, without significant changes or updates. This long lifecycle can lead to devices that are no longer supported by the manufacturer, with no mechanism for receiving patches or updates. Manufacturers may stop releasing security patches or software updates after a certain period, leaving these devices vulnerable to new threats. This creates a dilemma for organizations that rely on these devices— do they continue using the device with known vulnerabilities, or do they replace it with a more secure, but potentially more expensive, alternative? This issue is particularly problematic in industries such as healthcare or manufacturing, where legacy embedded systems are integral to critical operations, and replacing them can be costly and disruptive.

Security is a key concern when managing patches for IoT devices and embedded systems. Many IoT devices are deployed in environments where they handle sensitive data or control critical systems, making them attractive targets for cybercriminals. Vulnerabilities in these devices can be exploited to gain unauthorized access, exfiltrate data, or launch attacks on other connected systems. Unfortunately, many IoT devices are shipped with weak security settings, such as default passwords, hardcoded credentials, or outdated software. The lack of secure patching processes can leave these devices exposed to threats, especially when manufacturers fail to address known vulnerabilities in a timely manner. Given that these devices often operate continuously, the window of opportunity for an attacker is wide, and without proper patch management, the risks associated with unpatched vulnerabilities are significant.

One of the best practices for managing security patches in IoT and embedded systems is to establish a clear and consistent patching strategy before devices are deployed. Organizations should work closely with manufacturers to ensure that devices come with a defined lifecycle for patching and updates. This includes ensuring that the devices support secure update mechanisms, such as secure boot, encrypted firmware, and digital signatures, which can help ensure that patches are applied safely and without introducing additional vulnerabilities. Manufacturers should also provide a clear roadmap for the device's support period, outlining when patches will be available and when support will end. This information can help organizations plan for the eventual replacement of devices that are no longer supported and mitigate the risks associated with unsupported systems.

For devices already deployed in the field, remote patch management becomes critical. Many modern IoT devices are connected to the internet, which allows for remote updates. Organizations should leverage this connectivity to implement a system that can automatically push patches to devices. This can be done using a centralized patch management platform that can detect vulnerable devices and push the necessary updates remotely. However, the limited bandwidth and intermittent connectivity of some IoT devices make it essential for the patching system to be efficient and capable of handling low-bandwidth environments. Some devices may require scheduled updates that are deployed during low-traffic hours to avoid interfering with regular operations. The patch management system must also account for the device's limited resources, ensuring that patches are lightweight and optimized for performance.

Another essential strategy is monitoring and auditing. Even after patches have been deployed, continuous monitoring of IoT devices is necessary to ensure that they remain secure and functional. Vulnerabilities may arise over time due to new threats, misconfigurations, or unforeseen interactions between devices. Ongoing monitoring helps to identify when new patches are needed and whether the devices are still functioning as expected after an update. Auditing the patching process itself is also critical to ensure that patches are being applied properly and in a timely manner. Detailed records should be maintained to track which devices have been patched and when, and any failures should be logged and addressed immediately.

In some cases, organizations may also need to rely on third-party patching solutions to enhance their patch management capabilities. Third-party vendors may offer solutions that can help manage updates across a wide range of IoT devices from different manufacturers, streamlining the process and ensuring that all devices are up to date with the latest security patches. These solutions often include additional security features, such as vulnerability scanning and real-time alerting, which can help organizations stay on top of potential security risks.

Managing security patches for IoT devices and embedded systems is an ongoing challenge that requires a combination of proactive planning, efficient tools, and ongoing monitoring. Organizations must address the complexities of limited resources, remote deployments, and long lifecycles to ensure that their IoT devices remain secure and functional. By implementing a robust patch management strategy that includes secure update mechanisms, remote patching, and continuous monitoring, organizations can reduce the risk of security breaches and ensure that their IoT and embedded systems continue to support business operations safely and efficiently.

Ensuring Compatibility Between Patches and Existing Software

In the world of IT infrastructure management, one of the most significant challenges that organizations face is ensuring compatibility between newly released patches and the existing software and systems in their environment. Patches, which are intended to fix vulnerabilities, enhance system functionality, or resolve bugs, must be applied effectively to ensure that they do not disrupt other components of the system or create new problems. The complexity of modern IT environments, with their multitude of applications, devices, and operating systems, makes ensuring compatibility a critical task that requires careful planning, testing, and validation. Failure to do so can result in system outages, performance degradation, or even security vulnerabilities, undermining the very purpose of patching.

When a patch is released by a software vendor, it is usually designed to address specific security vulnerabilities or bugs that have been identified in the product. However, the installation of a patch may not always be straightforward, especially in complex environments where different versions of software, operating systems, and applications are in use. This diversity can introduce compatibility issues, where the patch might cause conflicts with existing configurations, applications, or dependencies. For instance, a patch that fixes a security vulnerability in a web server may unintentionally cause issues with database connectivity or interrupt the functionality of a web application that relies on that server. Similarly, a patch for an operating system may introduce compatibility problems with certain device drivers or other software packages, causing unexpected crashes or performance issues.

The primary reason for these compatibility challenges is that modern systems are made up of a wide variety of interconnected components. Each software update or patch may interact differently with these components, and testing every possible interaction can be extremely time-consuming and resource-intensive. Even minor changes in one area of the system can have far-reaching effects elsewhere. Moreover, some patches may be designed for specific versions of software, while other systems may be running older or custom-built versions that are not compatible with the patch. This problem is compounded by the fact that many organizations use a mix of proprietary, open-source, and third-party applications, each with its own patching schedule and compatibility requirements.

One of the most effective ways to address compatibility issues between patches and existing software is through thorough testing. Testing patches before they are deployed across the organization is a crucial step in ensuring that they will not cause disruptions or compatibility problems. This process involves applying the patch in a test environment that mirrors the production environment as closely as possible. By simulating real-world conditions, IT teams can observe how the patch interacts with the various components of the system, such as applications, operating systems, and hardware. In addition to checking for functional issues, testing should also include performance assessments to ensure that the patch does not degrade system performance or introduce any new vulnerabilities.

Another key aspect of testing is regression testing, which involves verifying that the patch does not negatively affect the existing functionality of the system. When a patch is applied, it may inadvertently change the behavior of certain components, leading to broken features or application failures. Regression testing helps identify such issues by testing the core functionality of the system after the patch has been applied. This process is especially important in environments with critical business applications, where even a minor disruption can have significant operational consequences. By performing thorough regression tests, organizations can identify potential issues before the patch is deployed to the live environment, reducing the risk of service interruptions.

In addition to testing, it is important to prioritize patches based on the potential impact they will have on the system. Not all patches are of equal importance, and some may be more likely to cause compatibility problems than others. Security patches, for example, are often given the highest priority, as they address vulnerabilities that could be exploited by attackers. However, these patches may also require more careful consideration, as they may introduce changes to system behavior or require updates to other software components to maintain compatibility. Non-security patches, such as performance improvements or bug fixes, may still be important but can often be deployed with less urgency. A well-defined patch prioritization strategy can help organizations manage the risks associated with patching by ensuring that the most critical patches are applied first, while allowing for more time to address potential compatibility issues with less critical patches.

A comprehensive patch management policy should also include a clear communication plan to ensure that all relevant stakeholders are aware of upcoming patches and their potential impact on existing software. Effective communication is essential to ensuring that everyone involved in the patching process is on the same page and understands the potential risks and benefits of applying a given patch. This includes notifying IT staff, system administrators, developers, and end-users about the patching schedule, the systems that will be affected, and any changes in system behavior or functionality that may occur as a result of the patch. By maintaining clear lines of communication, organizations can ensure that patches are applied smoothly and that any compatibility issues are addressed promptly.

For organizations that operate in complex, multi-platform environments, using centralized patch management tools can be extremely beneficial. These tools can automate much of the patching process, including detecting missing patches, scheduling deployments, and verifying that patches are applied correctly. Many patch management solutions also include compatibility checks, which can help identify potential issues before patches are deployed. These tools can be configured to apply patches to different systems based on their version, configuration, or criticality, ensuring that each system receives the appropriate patch in a way that minimizes the risk of compatibility problems. In environments where multiple vendors and software platforms are used, centralized patch management tools can provide a unified view of the patch status across the entire IT infrastructure, making it easier to track which patches have been applied and which still need to be addressed.

In addition to centralized tools, organizations should consider maintaining detailed inventories of their software and hardware components. This inventory should include information about the specific versions of software, configurations, and any customizations that have been made to the system. Having a clear understanding of the components in use allows IT teams to assess the compatibility of patches more effectively, as they can determine whether the patch is appropriate for the specific version of the software or hardware in question. Keeping an up-to-date inventory also helps streamline the testing and deployment process, as it provides IT teams with the information they need to ensure that patches are applied correctly and that any potential conflicts are identified and addressed in advance.

Ensuring compatibility between patches and existing software is a complex but essential aspect of patch management. By adopting a comprehensive approach that includes testing, prioritization, communication, centralized tools, and proper inventory management, organizations can reduce the risks associated with patching and ensure that their systems remain secure and functional. The goal is not only to apply patches promptly but also to do so in a way that minimizes disruption, maintains compatibility, and ensures that system performance remains optimal. In today's fast-paced IT landscape, this balance is critical to maintaining a secure, stable, and efficient technology environment.

Managing Third-Party Software Patches and Updates

In today's complex IT environments, third-party software plays a crucial role in the functionality and efficiency of business operations. From productivity tools and customer relationship management (CRM) systems to specialized industry software, organizations rely on a wide range of third-party applications to meet their needs. While these tools bring immense value, they also introduce specific challenges, particularly when it comes to patch management. Unlike first-party software, which is developed and maintained by the organization itself or a dedicated vendor, third-party software requires a more hands-on approach for managing patches and updates. Ensuring that third-party software is consistently updated and secure is a critical component of an organization's overall cybersecurity strategy, as vulnerabilities in third-party applications can lead to serious security breaches and operational disruptions.

One of the primary challenges in managing third-party software patches is the sheer number of applications that may be in use across an organization. Many businesses rely on a diverse range of third-party tools, each with its own patching schedule and update process. Some software vendors release patches regularly, while others may only release updates sporadically. As a result, organizations must monitor a wide array of vendors and applications to ensure that patches are applied in a timely and consistent manner. This can be particularly challenging in larger organizations or those using a wide variety of applications, as tracking updates across numerous platforms can quickly become overwhelming. Without a centralized system for patch management, it becomes difficult to keep track of which third-party applications need updates and which patches have been applied.

Another issue is that the patching process for third-party software is often outside of the organization's direct control. While first-party software typically provides direct communication channels and update mechanisms, third-party software requires organizations to depend on the vendor's release cycle and patching strategy. This introduces a level of uncertainty, as some vendors may not release patches immediately when vulnerabilities are discovered, leaving organizations exposed to potential risks. Additionally, some third-party vendors may not provide patch notifications or may not release detailed information about the patch's contents, making it difficult for organizations to assess the urgency of the patch or determine how it will impact existing systems. Organizations need to build relationships with third-party vendors to ensure timely notification of security patches and updates, and in cases where vendors fail to release timely patches, organizations must find alternative ways to mitigate the risks posed by unpatched software.

Security patches are particularly important when managing third-party software, as vulnerabilities in these applications can serve as entry points for cybercriminals. Third-party software, especially widely used applications, is often targeted by hackers due to the large attack surface they present. Many high-profile cyber-attacks have exploited vulnerabilities in popular third-party applications, leading to significant data breaches and financial losses. For example, unpatched vulnerabilities in widely used applications like Adobe Flash, Java, and web browsers have been the targets of numerous cyber-attacks over the years. Organizations must ensure that they not only keep third-party software updated but also conduct regular vulnerability assessments and penetration tests to identify and mitigate potential security risks. Failure to manage third-party software patches effectively can expose an organization to significant risks, especially as attackers become increasingly sophisticated in their targeting of vulnerable third-party applications.

To address these challenges, organizations should implement a robust and proactive third-party patch management strategy. One of the first steps in managing third-party software patches is to maintain a comprehensive inventory of all third-party applications in use across the organization. This inventory should include details such as the software version, the vendor, the update schedule, and any known vulnerabilities. By keeping an up-to-date inventory, organizations can more easily track which applications need patches and ensure that no software is overlooked. Additionally, organizations should regularly review and audit the inventory to identify any outdated or unsupported third-party applications. If a particular third-party software vendor discontinues support for a product or ceases to release patches, organizations should consider upgrading to a more secure alternative or implementing additional security measures to protect against potential vulnerabilities.

Once the inventory is established, organizations should prioritize patching based on the criticality of the application and the risks associated with unpatched vulnerabilities. Security patches for third-party applications should always take precedence, particularly if the application handles sensitive data or is integral to business operations. For example, a patch for a payment processing system or customer database application should be applied as quickly as possible to prevent data breaches or financial fraud. Similarly, organizations should assess the potential impact of a patch on their systems. For instance, a patch that addresses a security vulnerability but could cause compatibility issues with other critical software should be thoroughly tested before deployment. A risk-based approach to patch prioritization ensures that resources are allocated effectively and that the most critical issues are addressed first.

To ensure the patching process is efficient, organizations should leverage automated patch management tools that can help streamline the process of identifying, tracking, and deploying patches for third-party software. These tools can be configured to automatically check for available updates, schedule deployments, and verify that patches have been successfully applied. By automating these tasks, organizations can reduce the manual effort required to manage third-party patches, minimize the risk of human error, and ensure that patches are applied consistently across all systems. Automated tools can also integrate with vulnerability scanners to help identify unpatched vulnerabilities in third-party applications, making it easier to track and address security gaps.

While automation plays a significant role in third-party patch management, it is also important for organizations to thoroughly test patches before deploying them to production systems. Patch testing helps ensure that the updates will not cause disruptions, conflicts, or performance issues. For example, patches for third-party applications may conflict with custom configurations or integrations that have been made to meet specific business needs. A controlled testing environment should replicate the production environment as closely as possible to ensure that the patch will not negatively impact existing systems. Only after thorough testing and validation should patches be rolled out to the live environment. This step is especially critical when dealing with mission-critical third-party applications that cannot afford extended downtime or service interruptions.

In addition to testing and automation, effective communication is vital when managing third-party patches. IT teams should establish clear communication channels with third-party vendors to ensure they are promptly notified of security patches and updates. Regular communication with vendors can also help clarify patch details, such as what vulnerabilities the patch addresses, how it affects system functionality, and whether there are any known issues. By staying in close contact with vendors, organizations can proactively address potential patching issues before they become critical problems.

Managing third-party software patches requires a combination of proactive monitoring, strategic planning, automation, and communication. By maintaining an inventory of all third-party applications, prioritizing patches based on risk, leveraging automated patch management tools, and conducting thorough testing, organizations can ensure that third-party software remains secure and up to date. In today's interconnected world, where vulnerabilities in third-party applications are often exploited to gain unauthorized access to systems, it is essential for organizations to adopt a comprehensive and systematic approach to third-party patch management. By doing so, they can mitigate security risks, ensure compliance with regulatory requirements, and maintain the integrity of their IT infrastructure.

Risk-Based Prioritization of Patches

The application of patches is a vital part of maintaining secure and stable IT systems, but in today's complex environments, it is not always feasible to apply every patch immediately after it is released. With the rapid pace of software development and the growing number of vulnerabilities being discovered each year, organizations are faced with the challenge of managing a large number of patches for their systems, applications, and devices. As a result, effective patch management strategies must include a risk-based approach to prioritize patches. Risk-based prioritization helps organizations focus their resources on addressing the most critical vulnerabilities first, while minimizing the impact on system performance, business operations, and security. By assessing the risks associated with each patch, organizations can make informed decisions about which patches to apply immediately, which to schedule for later deployment, and which to defer or ignore entirely.

A risk-based approach to patch prioritization begins with assessing the severity of the vulnerabilities addressed by each patch. Vulnerabilities can vary widely in terms of their potential impact. Some may be relatively minor issues that have little to no effect on system performance or security, while others may represent significant threats that could allow attackers to gain unauthorized access to sensitive data, disrupt business operations, or cause financial losses. By evaluating the severity of each vulnerability, organizations can prioritize patches that address the most critical security flaws. This approach ensures that the most pressing risks are mitigated first, protecting the organization from the most dangerous threats. For example, a patch that addresses a vulnerability in a public-facing web server or a system that handles sensitive customer data would typically take precedence over a patch for a less critical system or internal application.

In addition to severity, the likelihood of exploitation is another important factor in risk-based prioritization. Not all vulnerabilities are equally likely to be exploited by cybercriminals or other malicious actors. Some vulnerabilities are well-known and actively targeted by attackers, while others are more obscure and less likely to be exploited in the short term. A vulnerability that is actively being exploited in the wild, or for which exploit code is publicly available, should be prioritized for immediate patching. These vulnerabilities pose an immediate risk to the organization and require swift action to mitigate the threat. On the other hand, vulnerabilities that are less likely to be exploited in the near term may be deferred or scheduled for later deployment, especially if they are low-impact issues that do not pose a significant risk to the organization's security posture.

Another critical element of risk-based prioritization is the potential impact of a vulnerability on the organization's operations. Some vulnerabilities may affect systems or applications that are critical to business operations, while others may impact non-essential systems. For instance, a vulnerability in a customer-facing e-commerce platform or a system that manages financial transactions could have a significant impact on an organization's ability to conduct business. In contrast, a vulnerability in an internal administrative application or non-production system may have little to no effect on day-to-day operations. When prioritizing patches, organizations must consider the potential business impact of a vulnerability and give higher priority to patches that address risks to mission-critical systems. By doing so, organizations can reduce the likelihood of operational disruptions or service outages that could affect customers, employees, or partners.

The risk-based approach to patch prioritization should also take into account the organization's existing security controls and defenses. Some systems may already have protective measures in place that mitigate the risk associated with a particular vulnerability. For example, a vulnerability in an internal database may not be as high risk if the system is protected by strong access controls, encryption, and monitoring. Similarly, firewalls, intrusion detection systems, and antivirus software may provide additional layers of protection that reduce the likelihood of a successful exploit. In such cases, a patch addressing the vulnerability may still be important but may not need to be applied immediately if the existing security controls are effective at preventing exploitation. However, if the security controls are inadequate or there are gaps in coverage, the patch should be prioritized to address the vulnerability as soon as possible.

Another factor to consider when prioritizing patches is the ease of deployment and potential for system disruption. Some patches may be relatively simple to apply, with minimal risk of causing system instability or downtime, while others may require significant testing, compatibility checks, or system reboots. In environments with critical systems or high availability requirements, patches that require downtime should be carefully planned and scheduled to minimize disruption to business operations. Organizations may also need to coordinate with other teams, such as development or operations, to ensure that the patching process does not interfere with ongoing projects or workflows. By taking into account the deployment complexity and potential disruption caused by applying a patch, organizations can prioritize patches that are easier to deploy and minimize the risk of service interruptions.

The age of the vulnerability also plays a role in risk-based patch prioritization. Vulnerabilities that have been present for an extended period may be less likely to be exploited, as attackers may have already targeted them or lost interest in exploiting the flaw. However, older vulnerabilities may still be critical, especially if they have been publicly disclosed or are associated with widely used software. In some cases, vulnerabilities that are more than a year old may still be exploited, particularly if a patch has not been applied to a large number of systems. Organizations should not assume that older vulnerabilities are inherently less risky but should instead evaluate each vulnerability based on its exposure, the availability of exploit tools, and the potential consequences of an attack.

A comprehensive risk-based prioritization strategy also requires ongoing monitoring and reassessment. As new threats emerge and new vulnerabilities are discovered, the organization's risk landscape may change. The prioritization of patches should be flexible and adaptable, allowing organizations to adjust their patching schedules in response to evolving threats. Vulnerability management tools and threat intelligence feeds can provide valuable information to help organizations stay up to date on the latest security risks and vulnerabilities. Regular vulnerability scanning, penetration testing, and security assessments can also help identify new vulnerabilities that may require immediate patching or remediation.

Finally, communication is a critical aspect of risk-based patch prioritization. IT and security teams must work closely together to assess vulnerabilities, prioritize patches, and deploy updates. Clear communication with other stakeholders, such as management, users, and external partners, is essential to ensure that patching efforts are aligned with business objectives and security priorities. By fostering collaboration and ensuring that everyone understands the risks and benefits of patch deployment, organizations can create a culture of proactive patch management that reduces the likelihood of security breaches and system failures.

Risk-based prioritization of patches is a key strategy for ensuring the security and stability of IT systems in today's rapidly changing technological landscape. By assessing the severity, likelihood, impact, and ease of deployment of patches, organizations can focus their efforts on addressing the most critical vulnerabilities first. This approach not only helps mitigate security risks but also minimizes operational disruptions and ensures that resources are allocated effectively. As organizations continue to face an ever-growing number of vulnerabilities and cyber threats, risk-based patch prioritization will remain an essential tool in their cybersecurity toolkit.

Patch Management in Highly Regulated Industries

In highly regulated industries such as healthcare, finance, and government, patch management is not just a matter of best practice—

it is a legal and operational imperative. These industries often deal with sensitive data, critical systems, and high-value assets that make them prime targets for cybercriminals. Ensuring that systems are kept secure and up to date with the latest patches is vital to comply with strict regulations, protect sensitive information, and maintain the trust of clients and stakeholders. However, patch management in these industries comes with unique challenges, as organizations must balance the need for timely patching with the demands of regulatory compliance, system uptime, and business continuity.

One of the most significant challenges for organizations in highly regulated industries is the need to comply with industry-specific regulations that mandate secure systems and data protection. For example, in the healthcare sector, organizations must adhere to the Health Insurance Portability and Accountability Act (HIPAA), which requires that systems be regularly updated and maintained to protect patient information. Similarly, the financial industry must comply with the Payment Card Industry Data Security Standard (PCI DSS), which requires organizations to apply security patches in a timely manner to safeguard payment card data. These regulations often specify that security patches must be applied within a set timeframe, such as within 30 days of release, to mitigate vulnerabilities that could lead to data breaches or unauthorized access to sensitive information.

Failure to comply with these regulatory requirements can result in severe penalties, including fines, legal action, and loss of business. In some cases, non-compliance can lead to reputational damage, loss of clients, and an erosion of trust. For example, if a healthcare organization fails to apply a security patch for a vulnerability in its electronic health record (EHR) system, it could expose patient data to unauthorized access, leading to a breach of HIPAA regulations. Similarly, if a financial institution neglects to patch a vulnerability in its online banking system, it could expose customers' financial data to theft, potentially violating PCI DSS requirements. Therefore, organizations in highly regulated industries must develop a patch management strategy that ensures timely patching while maintaining compliance with the applicable regulations.

Another challenge of patch management in highly regulated industries is the need to maintain system uptime and business continuity. Many of the systems in these industries are mission-critical and must remain operational at all times. For example, healthcare organizations rely on EHR systems, diagnostic equipment, and patient monitoring systems that must remain available to ensure patient care. Similarly, financial institutions rely on payment processing systems, trading platforms, and banking applications that must be operational 24/7 to serve customers and conduct business. In such environments, patching can be a complex and risky process, as applying a patch could potentially cause downtime or disrupt system functionality.

To address this challenge, organizations must develop a patch management process that minimizes the risk of downtime and ensures that patches are applied with minimal disruption to business operations. One approach is to deploy patches in stages, starting with non-production systems and gradually moving to production systems once the patch has been tested and validated. This staged approach allows organizations to identify potential issues with the patch before it affects critical systems, ensuring that any problems can be addressed in a controlled environment. Additionally, organizations can schedule patching during off-hours or during maintenance windows to minimize the impact on end-users and business operations. Some organizations also implement redundant systems or failover mechanisms to ensure that critical systems remain operational while patches are being applied.

In highly regulated industries, patch management must also account for the complexity of legacy systems and custom-built applications. Many organizations in these sectors rely on older technologies that may not be compatible with the latest patches or security updates. These legacy systems can present significant challenges, as they may lack vendor support or have custom configurations that require specialized patching procedures. Additionally, some of these systems may be so deeply embedded in the organization's operations that replacing them with newer technologies is not a viable option. As a result, organizations must develop tailored patch management strategies for legacy systems that take into account their unique requirements and potential risks.

For example, an organization in the healthcare sector may rely on an older imaging system that does not support the latest security patches.

In such cases, the organization must work closely with the vendor or third-party providers to develop custom solutions that address security vulnerabilities in the system. This may involve applying custom patches, implementing compensating security controls, or isolating the system from the broader network to reduce its exposure to threats. Regardless of the approach, patch management for legacy systems requires careful planning and coordination to ensure that these systems remain secure and compliant with industry regulations.

Effective patch management in highly regulated industries also requires robust auditing and documentation processes. Regulations such as HIPAA and PCI DSS require organizations to maintain detailed records of patching activities, including the identification of vulnerabilities, the patches applied, and the dates of deployment. These records must be readily accessible for audits and inspections by regulatory bodies. Auditing and documentation processes also help organizations track their patching progress, identify areas for improvement, and ensure that patches are being applied consistently across all systems. By maintaining accurate records, organizations can demonstrate compliance with regulatory requirements and provide evidence of their efforts to protect sensitive data and maintain secure systems.

In addition to meeting regulatory requirements, patch management in highly regulated industries must also address the evolving nature of cybersecurity threats. The threat landscape is constantly changing, with new vulnerabilities being discovered regularly and cybercriminals developing increasingly sophisticated attack methods. To stay ahead of these threats, organizations must implement a proactive patch management strategy that includes regular vulnerability assessments, threat intelligence feeds, and security monitoring. This proactive approach helps organizations identify potential risks before they become critical issues, ensuring that patches are applied as soon as they become available.

Collaboration between IT teams, security teams, and compliance officers is essential for ensuring effective patch management in highly regulated industries. IT and security teams must work together to identify vulnerabilities, test patches, and deploy updates across the organization's infrastructure. Compliance officers play a key role in ensuring that the patching process meets regulatory requirements and that the organization can demonstrate compliance during audits. Regular communication and coordination between these teams help ensure that patch management is aligned with both security objectives and regulatory obligations.

In highly regulated industries, patch management is not simply about applying patches; it is about doing so in a way that maintains compliance, protects sensitive data, and ensures business continuity. The process must be carefully planned and executed to minimize disruption, address vulnerabilities in legacy systems, and meet the requirements of regulatory bodies. By adopting a comprehensive and proactive patch management strategy, organizations in highly regulated industries can protect their systems, maintain compliance, and reduce the risk of cyber-attacks that could compromise their operations and reputation.

The Role of Patch Management in Business Continuity Planning

Business continuity planning (BCP) is a critical aspect of an organization's risk management strategy, designed to ensure that essential operations can continue in the face of disruptions, whether from natural disasters, cyberattacks, or system failures. A central component of a successful business continuity plan is the protection of the organization's IT systems, which often form the backbone of daily operations. Patch management plays a significant role in this process, as vulnerabilities in software and systems can lead to security breaches, data loss, or even complete operational shutdowns. By ensuring that all systems are up to date with the latest patches, organizations reduce the likelihood of these vulnerabilities being exploited and increase their ability to maintain continuous operations during times of crisis.

The first way patch management contributes to business continuity is by mitigating the risks posed by unpatched vulnerabilities. Security patches are typically released in response to identified weaknesses in software that could be exploited by malicious actors. Cyberattacks, such as ransomware, data breaches, and denial-of-service attacks, often target these vulnerabilities. When a vulnerability is left unpatched, it becomes an open door for attackers to infiltrate systems, steal sensitive information, or disrupt operations. The application of patches reduces the attack surface of an organization's IT infrastructure, making it more difficult for attackers to exploit known vulnerabilities. In the context of business continuity, keeping systems patched ensures that these potential entry points are closed, helping to safeguard critical business functions and reduce the impact of security incidents.

In addition to security vulnerabilities, patch management also plays a role in ensuring that systems remain functional and stable. Many patches are not solely security-related; they also address bugs, performance issues, and compatibility problems that could disrupt business operations. In a rapidly changing business environment, where downtime can result in lost productivity, revenue, or customer trust, keeping systems updated is crucial for maintaining system reliability. For example, patches for operating systems or core applications may fix bugs that cause system crashes or slow performance. By ensuring that systems are free from known bugs and software malfunctions, patch management helps to ensure the reliability and stability of business operations. This is particularly important in environments that rely on real-time data processing, financial transactions, or communication systems, where even minor issues can lead to significant disruptions.

Another important aspect of patch management in the context of business continuity is its impact on compliance and regulatory requirements. Many industries, particularly those in healthcare, finance, and government, are subject to strict regulations regarding the security and integrity of their IT systems. These regulations often require organizations to implement specific security measures, including the timely application of security patches to protect sensitive data and ensure operational resilience. Failure to comply with these regulations can lead to significant legal, financial, and reputational damage. A robust patch management process is essential for meeting these compliance requirements and demonstrating due diligence in safeguarding critical systems. In this sense, patch management is not only an IT issue but also a key component of an organization's broader compliance and risk management strategy, directly supporting its ability to maintain business continuity in a regulated environment.

The role of patch management becomes even more critical when considering the increasing complexity and interdependence of modern IT systems. In today's digital landscape, organizations rely on a wide variety of interconnected systems, from cloud platforms and enterprise applications to network devices and IoT systems. A single unpatched vulnerability in one part of the network can cascade, leading to widespread disruptions across the entire organization. This interconnectedness means that business continuity cannot be ensured by simply maintaining individual systems in isolation. A comprehensive patch management strategy must account for all components of the IT infrastructure and ensure that patches are applied consistently across the organization. This holistic approach helps to prevent vulnerabilities in one system from affecting others, ensuring that the organization can continue to operate smoothly even in the face of a cyber threat or technical failure.

Effective patch management also contributes to the organization's ability to recover quickly in the event of a disruption. In the event of a cyberattack, system failure, or other crisis, organizations must have a clear plan for how they will recover and restore operations. One of the key elements of this recovery process is ensuring that systems are patched and up to date, as vulnerabilities in unpatched systems could exacerbate the impact of the disruption or make recovery more difficult. A well-maintained patch management system ensures that systems are protected and that recovery efforts can be focused on restoring services, rather than addressing new security risks that may emerge during the recovery process. This can significantly reduce downtime and help the organization return to normal operations more quickly.

In order to align patch management with business continuity planning, organizations must adopt a proactive and coordinated approach. This requires regular assessments of the organization's IT infrastructure to identify critical systems that must be prioritized for patching. In many cases, mission-critical systems such as financial transaction platforms, customer relationship management (CRM) systems, or enterprise resource planning (ERP) systems should be patched first, as vulnerabilities in these systems could have the most significant impact on the business. At the same time, non-critical systems that are not essential to daily operations may be patched at a later time, provided that they do not pose an immediate security risk. Prioritization should also take into account the severity of the vulnerabilities being addressed, the likelihood of exploitation, and the potential impact on business operations. This risk-based approach ensures that resources are allocated efficiently and that the most critical systems are protected first.

Automation is a key tool in ensuring that patch management is integrated effectively into business continuity planning. In large organizations with diverse systems, manually tracking and applying patches can be time-consuming and error-prone. Automated patch management systems can help streamline this process by automatically identifying missing patches, scheduling deployments, and verifying that patches have been applied correctly. Automation reduces the risk of human error, ensures that patches are applied consistently, and speeds up the process, all of which are critical for minimizing disruptions and maintaining system security. Automated systems can also generate alerts and reports that provide real-time visibility into the status of patching efforts, helping IT teams track progress and ensure that critical patches are not overlooked.

While automation is important, patch testing is another essential component of ensuring business continuity during patch management. Deploying patches without adequate testing can introduce new issues or conflicts that disrupt business operations. Therefore, patches should be tested in a controlled environment that mirrors the production system as closely as possible. This allows IT teams to assess the impact of the patch on system functionality, performance, and security before it is deployed to live systems. Patch testing helps identify potential conflicts, bugs, or regressions, ensuring that the patch does not cause disruptions when applied to critical systems.

The integration of patch management with business continuity planning is essential for reducing the risk of system downtime, data loss, and operational disruptions. By adopting a proactive, coordinated approach to patch management that includes prioritization, automation, testing, and alignment with compliance requirements, organizations can protect their IT systems, reduce security risks, and ensure continuous operations. Patch management plays a vital role in safeguarding critical business functions, enabling organizations to remain resilient in the face of technological challenges and external threats.

Communicating Patch Management Strategies to Stakeholders

Effective communication is a key component of successful patch management, particularly when it comes to conveying strategies and decisions to various stakeholders within an organization. The patching process is integral to maintaining system security, operational efficiency, and compliance with regulatory standards, but it can often involve complex technical procedures that require clear communication across multiple departments. Stakeholders, including IT teams, management, compliance officers, and end-users, all need to understand how patches impact their respective areas of responsibility, and it is essential that organizations have well-defined strategies for keeping everyone informed and aligned.

The first step in communicating patch management strategies to stakeholders is identifying who needs to be involved in the communication process. Different stakeholders have different concerns and areas of interest. For example, IT teams and system administrators are primarily concerned with the technical aspects of patch deployment, such as identifying vulnerabilities, testing patches, and ensuring that systems are updated without causing disruptions. On the other hand, management may be more interested in the operational impact of patching, such as downtime, cost implications, and potential disruptions to business processes. Compliance officers need to be informed about patching schedules and how patches align with regulatory requirements. End-users, while not directly involved in the patching process, need to understand how patches may affect their work, including potential system downtime or changes to functionality.

Once the relevant stakeholders have been identified, the next step is to tailor the communication to their specific needs and concerns. For IT teams, communication should focus on the technical details of the patching process, such as which vulnerabilities the patches address, how patches will be tested, and when deployment will occur. For management, it is important to communicate the strategic importance of patching, including how it contributes to reducing security risks, ensuring business continuity, and maintaining compliance with industry regulations. Management may also be concerned with resource allocation, project timelines, and the potential impact of patching on business operations, so it is important to communicate the business case for timely patching and any mitigation plans for minimizing disruption. Compliance officers need clear and concise information about how patching efforts align with relevant regulations and industry standards, along with documentation of patching activities that may be required for audits or reporting. End-users, meanwhile, require simple, clear communication about how patches may affect their work, such as system reboots or changes in application functionality.

One of the most effective ways to communicate patch management strategies is through regular, structured updates. These updates should be scheduled at key stages of the patching process, from initial planning to post-deployment. For IT teams, regular meetings or reports can help ensure that everyone is on the same page about which patches are being applied, when testing will occur, and when deployment will take place. These updates can also serve as a forum for addressing any technical concerns or challenges that arise during the patching process. For management, high-level reports or presentations should be provided that summarize the status of patching efforts, the risks associated with vulnerabilities, and the steps being taken to address them. These reports should highlight the impact of patching on business continuity and demonstrate how timely patching aligns with the organization's overall security strategy. Compliance officers can be kept informed through regular compliance reviews or meetings that track patching progress against regulatory requirements. These updates should include detailed records of patches applied, their relevance to specific regulations, and any challenges or delays encountered in meeting compliance deadlines.

End-users should also receive timely communication, particularly when patches are expected to affect their workflows. Regular announcements or emails that inform employees about scheduled patch deployments and expected downtimes can help minimize frustration and confusion. It is essential to ensure that end-users are aware of the reasons for the patching process, such as addressing security vulnerabilities or improving system performance. Additionally, communication should focus on what end-users need to do, if anything, during the patching process. For example, they may need to save their work before a scheduled update or log off their systems during certain hours. Providing clear instructions about what is expected of them helps to ensure that patching goes smoothly and minimizes disruptions to their daily tasks.

Another important aspect of effective communication is transparency. It is crucial for organizations to be open and transparent about the patch management process, including any potential risks or challenges that may arise. This includes being upfront about the potential for system downtime, delays in patch deployment, or compatibility issues that could affect certain applications or systems. Transparency helps build trust among stakeholders, particularly management and end-users, who may have concerns about the impact of patching on operations. By providing clear, honest communication about the patching process and its potential effects, organizations can mitigate any negative perceptions and ensure that everyone is prepared for the changes.

It is also important to communicate the rationale behind patching decisions. When patches are applied, stakeholders need to understand why certain patches were prioritized over others, how they align with the organization's risk management strategy, and how they contribute to long-term security and compliance goals. IT teams can explain how vulnerabilities are assessed and why certain patches are deemed critical, while management can be informed about the business risks of leaving vulnerabilities unaddressed. Compliance officers can be assured that the patching process is in line with industry regulations, and end-users can better understand the role of patching in maintaining secure and reliable systems. By communicating the reasoning behind patching decisions, organizations can ensure that all stakeholders understand the bigger picture and support the patching strategy.

Additionally, communication should include feedback loops that allow stakeholders to share their concerns or experiences with the patching process. For IT teams, this could involve post-deployment reviews to assess whether patches caused any unforeseen issues or disruptions. Management may want to provide feedback on the impact of patching on operations, such as any downtime that occurred during the deployment process. End-users can provide valuable insights into how patches affected their work, whether they encountered any issues, and what could be improved in future patching efforts. Collecting feedback from all stakeholders helps organizations refine their patch management strategy and make adjustments to improve future communication and deployment efforts.

In some cases, especially in larger organizations, it may be beneficial to create a patch management communication plan that outlines the process for informing stakeholders at each stage of the patching lifecycle. This plan should specify the frequency of updates, the channels of communication to be used (such as emails, meetings, or dashboards), and the types of information that need to be shared. By formalizing the communication process, organizations can ensure that all stakeholders are consistently informed and that no important details are overlooked.

Communicating patch management strategies effectively is essential to ensuring the success of the process and minimizing disruptions to business operations. By tailoring communication to the needs of different stakeholders, being transparent about the patching process, and providing clear instructions and feedback mechanisms, organizations can foster a collaborative approach to patch management. This approach not only helps to ensure that patches are applied in a timely and efficient manner but also strengthens the overall security posture and enhances business continuity. Effective communication builds trust, facilitates smoother patching processes, and helps organizations maintain secure and reliable systems.

Auditing and Monitoring Patch Deployment

Auditing and monitoring patch deployment are critical elements of a comprehensive patch management strategy. The patching process, while vital for securing systems and maintaining compliance with regulatory standards, involves complexities that require ongoing oversight to ensure effectiveness and avoid disruptions. Once patches are applied, organizations must not only track their deployment but also verify that the intended changes have been successfully implemented without introducing new issues. This dual focus on auditing and monitoring helps organizations stay on top of their patching efforts, address problems promptly, and ensure that systems remain secure and stable.

Auditing is an essential step in validating the patch deployment process. It involves reviewing the activities associated with patch application to ensure that the patches were applied correctly, to the appropriate systems, and in compliance with internal policies and regulatory requirements. Auditing provides transparency into the patching process and serves as documentation for compliance audits, where organizations must demonstrate that they have taken the necessary steps to secure their systems. This is particularly important in industries that are subject to strict regulatory standards, such as healthcare and finance, where failure to apply patches could lead to significant fines or legal consequences. By auditing patch deployment, organizations can prove that they are meeting their obligations and reducing the risk of data breaches or other security incidents.

The first component of patch deployment auditing is ensuring that patches have been successfully applied to all the relevant systems. Auditing should track each patch's deployment status, identifying which systems have received the patch and which have not. This ensures that no systems are left unpatched, which could expose the organization to unnecessary risks. The audit should also confirm that patches have been applied to the correct versions of software or hardware. For example, applying a patch intended for an earlier version of an operating system to a more recent version may result in system instability or performance issues. Auditing helps prevent these mistakes by cross-checking patch deployment records against system configurations.

Another key part of patch auditing is verifying that patches were deployed in accordance with predefined schedules and policies. Most organizations establish patch management policies that dictate when patches should be deployed, how they should be tested, and what steps need to be taken before and after deployment. Auditing ensures that these policies are adhered to, helping to avoid missed deadlines or unauthorized patch applications. If a patch is applied outside of the scheduled window, or if it deviates from the organization's patch management procedures, the audit process will flag these discrepancies, prompting further investigation. This is essential for maintaining consistency and accountability throughout the patching process.

In addition to auditing the technical aspects of patch deployment, organizations must also ensure that the deployment process complies with relevant regulatory standards. For industries such as healthcare, finance, and energy, compliance requirements often mandate the timely application of security patches to protect sensitive data and critical systems. Auditing patch deployment in these contexts involves reviewing whether patches are applied within the mandated timeframes and whether proper documentation is maintained to demonstrate compliance. Regulatory bodies often require that organizations provide evidence of patch management practices, including detailed records of patches applied, the systems they were applied to, and the results of any testing or validation processes. Regular audits ensure that organizations can meet these compliance requirements and avoid the risk of non-compliance.

While auditing ensures that patches are applied correctly and in compliance with regulations, monitoring plays an equally important role in tracking the ongoing health of systems after patches have been deployed. Monitoring patch deployment involves real-time tracking of systems to ensure that patches are functioning as intended and have not caused unintended side effects. Monitoring is an essential part of post-deployment validation, as it helps detect any issues that may arise after the patch is applied. For example, a patch that addresses a security vulnerability might inadvertently cause compatibility issues with other applications or reduce system performance. Monitoring tools can help identify these problems quickly so that they can be addressed before they impact business operations.

Effective monitoring involves using automated tools that can track patch status across a wide range of systems. These tools typically provide dashboards that show whether patches have been successfully applied, whether systems are up-to-date, and whether there are any unresolved vulnerabilities. The real-time visibility provided by these tools enables IT teams to act swiftly if any issues arise. For example, if a patch deployment fails or causes system instability, the monitoring system can trigger alerts, allowing IT teams to roll back the patch or apply a hotfix to resolve the issue. This proactive approach to monitoring helps to minimize the risk of disruptions, ensuring that systems remain secure and operational.

In addition to tracking patch status, monitoring tools can also be configured to perform vulnerability scans on systems after patches are applied. Vulnerability scanning helps identify whether the patch has successfully closed the security gap it was designed to address. In cases where a patch does not fully resolve the vulnerability or introduces new issues, the monitoring system can alert IT staff so that further remediation can be applied. Regular vulnerability scans are a critical part of the patch management lifecycle, as they ensure that patched systems do not remain exposed to risks.

Post-patch monitoring should also include performance monitoring. Some patches, particularly those that address system bugs or enhance functionality, can have an impact on system performance. Monitoring tools can track key performance indicators (KPIs) such as CPU usage, memory utilization, network traffic, and application response times. These metrics provide insights into how the patch is affecting the system and help detect any performance degradation that might occur after deployment. If performance issues are identified, IT teams can assess whether the patch is the cause or if other factors are contributing to the problem. This type of monitoring helps ensure that patches do not introduce new performance bottlenecks or system failures.

Auditing and monitoring also play an important role in improving future patch management practices. The data collected during audits and monitoring can be analyzed to identify patterns, common issues, or areas for improvement in the patching process. For example, if certain patches consistently fail to deploy successfully or cause compatibility issues with specific systems, the organization can adjust its patching strategy to address these problems. The insights gained from auditing and monitoring can also inform the development of more effective patching policies, ensuring that future deployments are more efficient and less likely to cause disruptions.

Collaboration between IT, security, and compliance teams is essential to ensure effective auditing and monitoring of patch deployment. Security teams should be involved in tracking vulnerabilities and ensuring that patches are addressing the right risks, while compliance teams ensure that the patching process aligns with regulatory requirements. Regular communication and coordination among these teams help streamline the auditing and monitoring process and ensure that any issues are promptly addressed.

Auditing and monitoring are essential components of a successful patch management strategy. By ensuring that patches are deployed correctly, in line with policies, and without causing disruptions, organizations can maintain secure and stable IT systems. Ongoing monitoring after patches are applied helps identify potential issues early and minimizes the risk of system downtime or security breaches. Together, auditing and monitoring provide the visibility, accountability, and control needed to maintain the integrity of IT systems and ensure that patch management is both effective and efficient.

Patch Management in Hybrid IT Environments

In today's increasingly complex IT landscape, organizations are adopting hybrid IT environments to leverage the benefits of both on-premises systems and cloud-based services. A hybrid IT environment typically combines traditional infrastructure with cloud computing, often using a mix of private and public clouds, as well as on-premises servers, applications, and data centers. While hybrid IT environments offer scalability, flexibility, and cost savings, they also introduce significant challenges for patch management. Managing patches across such diverse environments requires a strategic approach that ensures consistency, security, and compliance while minimizing downtime and operational disruptions. Effective patch management in a hybrid IT environment involves coordinating and automating patch deployment across multiple platforms, managing security vulnerabilities, and ensuring seamless integration between on-premises and cloud systems.

One of the primary challenges of patch management in hybrid IT environments is the complexity of managing patches across multiple platforms with varying architectures, configurations, and security requirements. On-premises systems often run traditional enterprise software and legacy applications, which may require specific patching procedures or configurations. In contrast, cloud-based services may involve a wide range of Software-as-a-Service (SaaS) applications, virtualized instances, and infrastructure managed by third-party providers. The differences between these systems—whether in terms of operating systems, software versions, or update mechanisms—complicate the patching process. Organizations must ensure that patches are applied to both on-premises systems and cloud-based services in a coordinated manner, ensuring that all components of the IT environment remain secure and compliant with internal policies and regulatory standards.

In a hybrid IT environment, patch management must also account for the shared responsibility model that exists between the organization and its cloud service providers. In the cloud, the responsibility for patching is often divided between the provider and the customer. For example, cloud providers typically handle the patching of the underlying infrastructure, such as the hardware, hypervisors, and operating systems that support cloud services. However, customers are responsible for patching their own applications, virtual machines, and data. This division of responsibilities requires clear communication and coordination between the organization and the cloud provider to ensure that patches are applied in a timely manner and that there are no gaps in security coverage. Failure to understand the shared responsibility model can lead to missed patches or miscommunication about who is responsible for patching specific components, leaving the organization vulnerable to security threats.

Another challenge is ensuring that patch management processes are standardized and consistent across both on-premises and cloud environments. In many organizations, the IT team uses different tools and platforms to manage patches for on-premises systems and cloud resources, leading to fragmentation in the patch management process. For example, patching tools designed for on-premises servers may not be compatible with cloud-based systems, requiring organizations to use multiple tools or manual processes to track and deploy patches across their hybrid infrastructure. This lack of integration between on-premises and cloud patching solutions can lead to inefficiencies, missed patches, and difficulty in maintaining an accurate view of the organization's patch status. To address this issue, organizations need to invest in unified patch management platforms that can manage patches across both on-premises and cloud environments. These platforms should provide centralized visibility into patch deployment, automate the process as much as possible, and ensure that patches are applied uniformly across all systems, regardless of their location or configuration.

In addition to addressing the technical challenges of patch management, organizations in hybrid IT environments must also consider the operational impact of patching on business continuity. In many cases, systems in hybrid environments support critical business functions, such as customer transactions, employee productivity, or data processing. Even minor disruptions during patching can lead to significant downtime or loss of productivity. To minimize the impact of patch deployment, organizations must develop a well-defined patching schedule that considers both the technical aspects of patch management and the operational needs of the business. This may involve scheduling patch deployments during off-peak hours, using rolling updates to apply patches incrementally, or leveraging redundant systems to ensure that critical services remain available while patches are applied. Furthermore, testing patches before deployment is essential to ensure that they do not cause unforeseen compatibility issues or performance degradation, particularly when applied to complex hybrid environments with interconnected systems.

One of the most critical aspects of patch management in hybrid IT environments is maintaining security across both on-premises and cloud-based systems. The ever-growing threat landscape, with increasingly sophisticated cyberattacks and vulnerabilities, makes patching a high-priority activity for organizations seeking to safeguard sensitive data and maintain business continuity. Vulnerabilities in one part of the hybrid infrastructure can have ripple effects throughout the entire system, especially in environments that rely on interconnected applications and services. For example, a vulnerability in an on-premises web server could be exploited by attackers to access cloud-based databases or other critical systems. To mitigate this risk, organizations must ensure that all components of their hybrid IT environment are continuously monitored for vulnerabilities and that patches are applied to close any gaps. This requires a proactive approach to vulnerability management, which includes regular scanning for known vulnerabilities, integrating threat intelligence feeds, and staying up to date with security advisories from both on-premises software vendors and cloud service providers.

Compliance is another significant consideration when managing patches in hybrid IT environments. Many industries, such as healthcare, finance, and government, are subject to strict regulations that require organizations to maintain secure systems and protect sensitive data. These regulations often mandate that patches be applied within a specific timeframe to address vulnerabilities and protect against data breaches or other security incidents. In hybrid environments, compliance can be more challenging, as organizations must ensure that both on-premises and cloud-based systems are updated in accordance with these requirements. This may involve maintaining detailed records of patch deployment, tracking compliance with specific regulations, and conducting regular audits to demonstrate that patching efforts meet regulatory standards. Given the complexity of hybrid IT environments, organizations must have robust processes in place to ensure that they can consistently apply patches and maintain compliance with applicable laws and regulations.

Automation is an essential tool for streamlining patch management in hybrid IT environments. The scale and complexity of hybrid infrastructures make manual patching inefficient and error-prone, especially when managing large numbers of systems spread across multiple locations and platforms. Automated patch management tools can help organizations identify missing patches, schedule patch deployment, and verify that patches have been successfully applied. These tools can also provide centralized visibility into the status of patch deployment across the entire infrastructure, enabling IT teams to quickly identify systems that are out of date or vulnerable to attack. Automation not only improves the efficiency and accuracy of patch management but also helps organizations stay on top of the constant stream of patches released by software vendors and cloud providers. By automating the patching process, organizations can reduce the risk of human error, minimize downtime, and ensure that systems remain secure and compliant.

Managing patch deployment in hybrid IT environments presents a range of technical, operational, and security challenges. From coordinating patching efforts between on-premises systems and cloud services to ensuring compliance with regulatory standards, organizations must adopt a strategic and coordinated approach to patch management. By leveraging automated tools, adopting unified patch management platforms, and maintaining a proactive security posture, organizations can effectively manage patches across their hybrid IT infrastructure. As the IT landscape continues to evolve, the importance of effective patch management in hybrid environments will only increase, making it a key component of any organization's cybersecurity and business continuity strategy.

The Role of Patch Management in Incident Response

In the realm of cybersecurity, incident response is a critical process that helps organizations detect, manage, and recover from security incidents or breaches. Effective incident response requires a well-coordinated strategy, clear communication, and the right tools to address a wide range of security events, including malware infections, data breaches, or system outages caused by vulnerabilities. One key element of incident response is patch management, which plays a significant role in both preventing incidents and mitigating their impact once they occur. Patches address known vulnerabilities in software, operating systems, and hardware, helping to close security gaps that could otherwise be exploited by attackers. As such, a robust patch management process is not only important for proactive security but also for a swift and effective incident response.

Patch management plays an integral role in preventing incidents before they occur. Many security breaches are the result of known vulnerabilities that remain unpatched for extended periods. Attackers frequently exploit these vulnerabilities to gain unauthorized access to systems, escalate privileges, or exfiltrate sensitive data. Patch management serves as a proactive measure to address these vulnerabilities before they can be exploited. By regularly updating systems with the latest patches, organizations can significantly reduce the risk of incidents caused by these known vulnerabilities. Furthermore, patching helps to minimize the window of opportunity for attackers. Vulnerabilities, once identified, often have a lifecycle during which they are actively targeted by cybercriminals. Timely patching ensures that systems are less likely to fall victim to these threats.

However, even with a strong patch management program in place, incidents may still occur due to vulnerabilities that were not yet discovered or that were missed during patching. This is where patch management becomes a crucial element of the incident response process. When a security incident is detected, one of the first actions the incident response team takes is to assess whether the systems affected by the incident are up-to-date with the latest patches. If vulnerabilities that could have been addressed by patches are found in the compromised systems, applying the relevant patches becomes an immediate priority. In this sense, patch management is not just a preventive measure but a critical response step that helps to contain and resolve incidents more effectively.

During an incident response, patch management becomes part of the containment and eradication phase. Once a system is compromised, the goal is to stop the attack from spreading and to remove the threat from the environment. If the root cause of the incident is linked to a known vulnerability, applying patches can prevent the attacker from exploiting the same vulnerability again. This helps to stop the attack in its tracks and prevent any further damage to the organization's systems or data. For example, if an attacker exploited a vulnerability in a web application to gain unauthorized access, the patching of the application can eliminate the flaw that was used for exploitation, reducing the likelihood of the attacker being able to access the system again. By applying patches during the incident response process, organizations can rapidly neutralize a threat and mitigate the potential damage caused by an attack.

Patch management also plays a crucial role in the recovery phase of incident response. Once an attack has been contained and eradicated, the next step is to restore affected systems to their normal state. During this phase, incident response teams will typically work to restore systems from backups, reconfigure security settings, and apply any necessary patches that may have been missed before the incident. By ensuring that all systems are fully patched during the recovery process, organizations can prevent future incidents from arising due to the same vulnerabilities. Furthermore, applying patches during recovery also serves as a way to improve the overall security posture of the organization, addressing any weaknesses that may have been previously overlooked or ignored. This comprehensive patching process ensures that systems are not only restored but are also better protected against future threats.

In the context of incident response, patch management also contributes to the lessons learned phase. After the incident is resolved, organizations conduct post-incident reviews to identify what went wrong, how the response was handled, and what could be improved for future incidents. Patch management is an important area of focus during these reviews. For example, incident responders may analyze whether unpatched vulnerabilities contributed to the breach and whether there were delays in patch deployment that allowed the attack to escalate. This analysis can help organizations identify weaknesses in their patch management process, such as inadequate patch testing, delayed deployments, or lack of visibility into patch status. By learning from these experiences, organizations can refine their patch management strategies to be more effective in preventing and responding to future incidents.

Collaboration between the incident response team and the IT or security team is essential to ensure that patch management is effectively integrated into the incident response process. In many organizations, the incident response team is responsible for detecting and analyzing security incidents, while the IT or security team is responsible for managing patches and updates. However, during an active incident, the two teams must work closely together to identify the vulnerabilities that need to be patched and to quickly deploy updates across affected systems. This collaboration ensures that patching is not delayed and that the incident response team has the support they need to mitigate the incident. Furthermore, IT teams should be prepared to deploy emergency patches or hotfixes during an ongoing incident to address critical vulnerabilities, especially if a patch is not yet available from the software vendor.

Automation is another important consideration in integrating patch management with incident response. Given the speed at which cyberattacks can unfold, incident response teams need to act quickly to apply patches and updates. Manual patching can be slow and error-prone, especially in large organizations with complex IT environments. Automation tools can help streamline the process by automatically identifying missing patches, prioritizing updates based on the severity of the vulnerabilities, and deploying patches in real-time. This allows organizations to respond faster to incidents, reducing the time it takes to mitigate threats and recover from attacks. Automated patching also ensures consistency across the organization, minimizing the risk of human error and ensuring that all systems are updated promptly.

One of the challenges of patch management in incident response is the potential impact of patches on system performance and business continuity. Some patches, particularly those that address critical vulnerabilities, may require system restarts or downtime, which could disrupt business operations. During an incident, patching systems while they are under active attack could also cause additional stress on already strained infrastructure. Therefore, careful consideration must be given to the timing and method of applying patches during an incident. In some cases, rolling updates or staged patch deployments may be necessary to avoid system overload or service interruptions. Incident response teams must be prepared to assess the risks associated with applying patches during an ongoing attack and ensure that patching activities do not inadvertently cause further issues.

Patch management in incident response is not just about applying patches during or after a security event; it is also about creating a proactive strategy to reduce vulnerabilities and improve the overall security posture of the organization. By ensuring that patching is an integral part of the incident response process, organizations can better defend against security breaches, reduce the impact of attacks, and enhance their ability to recover quickly. A well-coordinated patch management strategy within the context of incident response is essential for protecting critical systems, maintaining business continuity, and strengthening the organization's overall cybersecurity resilience.

The Impact of Unpatched Systems on Organizational Security

In today's fast-evolving digital landscape, patch management is an essential aspect of any organization's security strategy. However, despite the critical role patches play in securing IT systems, many organizations struggle to maintain up-to-date patches across all their systems. Unpatched systems, whether due to delays in applying updates or oversight, present a significant threat to organizational security. These unpatched systems often serve as entry points for attackers, making it easier for them to exploit known vulnerabilities and gain unauthorized access. The impact of unpatched systems can be far-reaching, affecting everything from data integrity to business continuity and organizational reputation. Understanding the dangers posed by unpatched systems is key to recognizing the importance of patch management in maintaining a robust security posture.

One of the primary risks associated with unpatched systems is the exposure to known vulnerabilities. Security patches are typically released by software vendors to fix identified vulnerabilities that could be exploited by attackers. These vulnerabilities, once discovered, often become public knowledge, and attackers quickly develop methods to exploit them. For instance, an attacker might exploit a vulnerability in an unpatched operating system to gain administrative access, steal sensitive data, or introduce malicious software into a network. Unpatched systems provide an open door for such attacks, as the vulnerabilities they contain remain unaddressed, allowing attackers to exploit them at will. The longer an organization delays patching, the higher the likelihood that these vulnerabilities will be targeted by cybercriminals.

The consequences of attacks on unpatched systems can be severe, leading to significant data breaches and financial losses. Cyberattacks, such as ransomware, are often launched through known vulnerabilities in unpatched systems. Once a vulnerability is exploited, attackers can take control of the system, encrypt valuable data, and demand payment for its release. These types of attacks can cripple an organization, causing operational downtime, loss of critical data, and potential damage to business relationships. In some cases, the cost of a ransomware attack can be astronomical, not only in terms of the ransom payment but also in the recovery efforts and legal liabilities associated with data loss or theft. The reputational damage from such incidents can be just as devastating, as customers and partners lose trust in the organization's ability to protect sensitive information.

Beyond the direct impact on data and financial resources, unpatched systems can also introduce long-term risks to organizational security. Once attackers gain access to an unpatched system, they can use it as a foothold to launch further attacks within the network. For example, an attacker may exploit a vulnerability in a seemingly insignificant system to gain access to more critical infrastructure, moving laterally within the network and escalating privileges along the way. This type of attack can be difficult to detect, as attackers often disguise their movements and actions within the system. As they gain deeper access, they may compromise other systems, steal more sensitive data, or disrupt critical business operations. The longer the unpatched vulnerability remains unaddressed, the more opportunities attackers have to escalate their attack and cause widespread damage.

Another significant issue associated with unpatched systems is the difficulty in maintaining compliance with industry regulations. Many industries, particularly those dealing with sensitive customer data, are subject to strict regulatory requirements regarding data protection, system security, and patching. For example, in healthcare, organizations must comply with the Health Insurance Portability and Accountability Act (HIPAA), which mandates timely patching of systems to ensure the protection of patient information. Similarly, in finance, the Payment Card Industry Data Security Standard (PCI DSS) requires businesses to keep systems up to date with the latest security patches to protect payment card data. Failing to patch systems in a timely manner can result in regulatory fines, legal penalties, and loss of certification. Furthermore, non-compliance with patching requirements can damage an organization's reputation, as customers and stakeholders may view the failure to protect systems as negligent or irresponsible.

The impact of unpatched systems also extends to business continuity. In today's interconnected world, organizations rely heavily on their IT infrastructure to conduct day-to-day operations. When systems are compromised due to unpatched vulnerabilities, the consequences can be felt across the entire organization. A single unpatched vulnerability in a critical system can lead to widespread disruptions, preventing employees from accessing necessary applications, causing delays in services, and halting business operations. In extreme cases, organizations may face days or even weeks of downtime while systems are restored and security breaches are addressed. The longer it takes to resolve these issues, the greater the impact on the organization's bottom line. Moreover, the disruption caused by security incidents can harm relationships with customers and partners, as they may lose confidence in the organization's ability to maintain operational stability.

Furthermore, unpatched systems can provide an entry point for more sophisticated attacks, including advanced persistent threats (APTs). APTs are stealthy, long-term cyberattacks that often target high-value systems within an organization. Attackers carrying out APTs typically gain access to a network through an unpatched system and maintain a presence within the network over an extended period. The goal of an APT is not only to steal data or cause immediate damage but also to establish ongoing access for future exploitation. By keeping systems unpatched, organizations provide attackers with the opportunity to install malware, create backdoors, or steal credentials that can be used for long-term surveillance or data theft. These types of attacks are often difficult to detect, and the longer the vulnerability remains unpatched, the more time attackers have to execute their plans.

In addition to the direct security risks, unpatched systems can also lead to increased operational costs. Addressing the aftermath of a security breach caused by an unpatched vulnerability often requires significant resources, both in terms of financial investment and human capital. Organizations may need to hire external cybersecurity experts to investigate the breach, contain the damage, and remediate vulnerabilities. Legal costs can also escalate, as organizations may face lawsuits from affected customers or penalties from regulatory bodies for failing to protect data adequately. The financial burden of responding to a breach can far exceed the cost of implementing a proper patch management strategy, which is far more cost-effective in the long run.

The impact of unpatched systems on organizational security extends far beyond the immediate risks of exploitation. Unpatched vulnerabilities provide attackers with easy entry points into an organization's network, potentially compromising critical data, disrupting business operations, and undermining trust with customers and stakeholders. These risks underscore the importance of maintaining an effective patch management strategy that addresses vulnerabilities promptly and consistently. By staying vigilant and ensuring that systems are regularly updated, organizations can safeguard against the threats posed by unpatched vulnerabilities and ensure the integrity and continuity of their operations.

Patch Management Best Practices for Small and Medium Enterprises

For small and medium enterprises (SMEs), effective patch management is crucial to maintaining secure, efficient, and reliable IT systems. With limited resources and often fewer dedicated IT staff compared to larger organizations, SMEs face unique challenges when it comes to patching their systems. However, neglecting patch management can expose these businesses to significant security risks, including data breaches, system failures, and reputational damage. Implementing best practices for patch management allows SMEs to mitigate these risks, comply with industry regulations, and ensure the ongoing stability of their IT infrastructure.

The first step in effective patch management for SMEs is developing a patch management policy. This policy should define the organization's approach to patching, outlining who is responsible for monitoring, testing, and deploying patches. Having a clear policy helps to ensure that patches are applied consistently and in a timely manner across the organization. For SMEs with smaller IT teams, the policy should prioritize the most critical systems and applications, ensuring that patching efforts are focused where they will have the most significant impact on security. The policy should also include guidelines for patch testing, approval, and deployment, with a focus on minimizing system downtime while addressing vulnerabilities effectively.

Given the limited resources often available to SMEs, automation plays a crucial role in patch management. Automated patch management tools can help SMEs streamline the patching process, reducing the manual effort required to track and apply updates. These tools can scan systems for missing patches, schedule updates, and even deploy patches automatically across multiple systems. By automating the patch management process, SMEs can ensure that patches are applied promptly and consistently without overburdening their IT staff. Automated tools also help to reduce the risk of human error, ensuring that critical patches are not missed or incorrectly applied.

In addition to automation, SMEs should leverage centralized patch management systems that provide visibility and control over the entire patching process. A centralized system allows SMEs to track the status of patch deployment across all systems, providing real-time insights into which patches have been applied and which systems are still vulnerable. These systems help IT teams prioritize patching efforts and monitor progress, ensuring that updates are applied systematically and without overlooking any critical systems. Centralized patch management solutions also provide comprehensive reporting capabilities, making it easier for SMEs to demonstrate compliance with industry regulations and internal security policies.

For SMEs, prioritization of patches is essential. Due to limited resources and the constant pressure to maintain business operations, it is not always feasible to patch every system or application at once. Therefore, SMEs must adopt a risk-based approach to patch management, prioritizing patches based on the criticality of the vulnerabilities they address. Patches for systems that are exposed to the internet, such as web servers, email servers, and customer-facing applications, should be given the highest priority, as these systems are most likely to be targeted by attackers. Patches that address vulnerabilities in mission-critical systems, such as financial or database servers, should also be prioritized to minimize potential disruptions to business operations. Less critical systems, such as internal tools or non-production systems, can be patched at a later stage, but they should still be included in the overall patching schedule.

Testing patches before deployment is another essential best practice for SMEs. While testing may seem time-consuming, it is critical to ensure that patches do not interfere with system functionality or performance. SMEs should set up a test environment that mirrors their production systems as closely as possible. This environment allows IT teams to evaluate the impact of patches before applying them to live systems, minimizing the risk of unexpected downtime or compatibility issues. While testing every patch may not be feasible for smaller businesses, it is especially important to test patches that address security vulnerabilities in critical systems or applications. A small investment in testing can help avoid larger issues down the road, such as system outages or data corruption caused by incompatible patches.

Maintaining an up-to-date inventory of all software and hardware assets is essential for effective patch management in SMEs. Without a comprehensive inventory, it can be difficult to track which systems require patches and which have already been updated. SMEs should maintain a detailed record of all software and hardware assets, including operating systems, applications, and network devices, along with their respective versions and patch levels. This inventory allows SMEs to quickly identify which systems are vulnerable to known threats and ensures that patching efforts are focused on the right systems. Furthermore, it helps organizations stay on top of vendor support lifecycles, ensuring that unsupported software or hardware is replaced before it becomes a security liability.

SMEs should also regularly monitor and audit the patch management process to ensure its effectiveness. Regular audits help to identify gaps in the patching process, such as missed patches or systems that are not receiving updates. These audits should be conducted on a regular basis, with a particular focus on critical systems and applications. Monitoring tools can help SMEs track patch deployment and alert IT teams to any issues that arise during the patching process. For example, if a patch fails to deploy successfully or if a system is not receiving updates as expected, monitoring tools can provide alerts that enable IT teams to take immediate action. Continuous monitoring and auditing help SMEs stay proactive in addressing security vulnerabilities and ensuring that their patch management practices are aligned with industry standards.

In highly regulated industries, patch management is not just about security—it is also about compliance. Many industries, such as healthcare, finance, and government, are subject to strict regulatory requirements regarding data protection and system security. These regulations often include specific guidelines for patch management, such as requirements for timely patching of critical vulnerabilities. For SMEs operating in these industries, patch management is an essential component of maintaining compliance with regulatory standards. A well-documented patch management process, combined with regular audits and reporting, helps SMEs demonstrate compliance to regulators and avoid costly penalties. Compliance with patching requirements also helps build trust with customers and partners, as it demonstrates a commitment to protecting sensitive data and maintaining secure systems.

Finally, SMEs should foster a culture of security awareness across the organization. Patch management is not just an IT responsibility—it is a business-wide concern. Employees at all levels should be aware of the importance of patching and the role it plays in safeguarding the organization's assets. Training programs can help staff understand the risks associated with unpatched systems and the need to follow security protocols, such as reporting vulnerabilities or potential security issues. A culture of security awareness ensures that everyone within the organization understands their role in maintaining a secure environment and contributes to the overall success of the patch management strategy.

Patch management for small and medium enterprises presents unique challenges, but with the right approach, it is possible to maintain secure, efficient, and compliant systems. By implementing best practices such as developing a patch management policy, leveraging automation, prioritizing patches, and regularly testing and auditing systems, SMEs can significantly reduce their exposure to security threats and improve their overall cybersecurity posture. Patch management is a critical element of an SME's broader risk management strategy, helping to protect systems, maintain business continuity, and ensure the trust of customers and stakeholders. By staying proactive and adopting a strategic approach to patching, SMEs can build a strong foundation for long-term success and security.

Automating Patch Rollbacks and Recovery Processes

In the realm of IT security and systems management, patches are essential for keeping systems secure and up-to-date, but the process of patching is not always straightforward. While patches are designed to fix vulnerabilities, improve functionality, or add features, they can also inadvertently cause issues. These issues may range from system crashes, application incompatibility, to degraded performance, making it crucial for organizations to have robust systems in place to quickly revert patches and restore functionality when things go wrong. Automating patch rollbacks and recovery processes ensures that organizations can minimize downtime, quickly address patching failures, and maintain business continuity in the face of unexpected issues.

When a patch is deployed, it is generally applied to enhance the security or performance of a system. However, there are instances when a patch does not function as expected. This could be due to compatibility issues with other applications, system configurations, or even bugs in the patch itself. If these issues are not quickly detected, they can cause significant disruptions to the organization's operations, resulting in system downtime, lost productivity, and in some cases, financial losses. Manual intervention in these situations can be slow, error-prone, and disruptive. In such circumstances, having an automated rollback and recovery mechanism in place allows organizations to restore systems to their previous, stable state much more quickly, minimizing the negative impact of patch-related failures.

Automating the patch rollback process begins with establishing a system that can detect when a patch has caused problems. The first step in this process is to have real-time monitoring tools that can continuously assess the state of systems after a patch is applied. These tools can track key performance indicators, system stability, and application functionality to detect anomalies or issues that arise post-patch. For example, if a patch leads to a critical application crash or significantly affects system performance, the monitoring tools can flag these issues immediately. Once the problem is identified, the automated rollback process can begin, reducing the need for manual intervention.

The rollback process involves reversing the changes introduced by the patch and restoring the system to its previous configuration. This is an essential step in ensuring that business operations can continue while the issues introduced by the patch are addressed. In an automated system, rollback processes can be pre-configured to run based on specific conditions. For example, if a critical vulnerability patch causes a system crash, the automated rollback mechanism can trigger the restoration of the previous system state without requiring human input. This ensures that users and business operations experience minimal disruption, as the system returns to a known stable state while IT teams investigate and resolve the issue with the patch.

The ability to quickly roll back patches is particularly important in organizations where system uptime is crucial. For example, in industries like healthcare, finance, and e-commerce, even a short period of system downtime can lead to significant operational and financial consequences. Automated patch rollback systems reduce the risk of such disruptions by ensuring that patches can be reverted quickly and efficiently. In environments with strict regulatory requirements, where compliance with data protection laws is essential, rapid rollback can also help organizations meet their legal obligations by restoring systems to a secure, compliant state.

Alongside the automated rollback mechanism, recovery processes are equally important. After a patch has been rolled back, systems must be restored to normal functioning. This recovery process involves not only restoring the patch itself but also ensuring that any other systems, applications, or services that were impacted by the failed patch are also fully operational. Automated recovery processes can be integrated with backup systems to restore affected systems from recent backups, ensuring that any changes made since the patch deployment are preserved. These recovery systems can be designed to operate with minimal intervention, automatically identifying and restoring backup versions of critical files or databases that may have been corrupted by the failed patch.

Automating both the rollback and recovery processes requires seamless integration with other IT systems, such as backup management, version control, and configuration management tools. Version control systems ensure that both patches and their rollback versions are tracked, providing a clear record of what changes were made and when. This is important not only for restoring systems but also for auditing purposes, as it enables IT teams to track the history of patch deployments and identify any patterns in patch failures. Similarly, configuration management systems help to ensure that all relevant configurations are restored during the recovery process, maintaining consistency and ensuring that the system is fully functional after rollback.

One of the challenges of automating patch rollbacks and recovery processes is ensuring that these systems are tested and validated regularly. While automation can speed up the process of detecting issues and restoring systems, it is crucial to thoroughly test the rollback and recovery procedures to ensure they work as intended. Automated rollback mechanisms should be periodically tested in a controlled environment to verify that they do not introduce additional issues or conflicts when reverting patches. This testing should simulate real-world conditions, where patches may fail due to unexpected interactions with other system components. By conducting these tests, organizations can identify potential weaknesses in their automated rollback and recovery processes and address them before they become critical during an actual incident.

The integration of artificial intelligence (AI) and machine learning (ML) can further enhance the automation of patch rollbacks and recovery. AI and ML can be used to predict potential issues before they occur by analyzing historical data on patch deployments and identifying patterns that are indicative of future failures. For example, if a certain type of patch or a specific system configuration is repeatedly associated with failures, AI systems can flag these patterns and help IT teams take preventive measures, such as avoiding certain patches or rolling them out gradually. This predictive capability can reduce the number of instances where a patch causes a failure and, in turn, decrease the need for rollbacks and recovery efforts.

Another advantage of automating patch rollbacks and recovery processes is the reduction of human error. Manual intervention during the patching process can lead to mistakes, such as improperly rolling back patches or failing to restore critical systems correctly. Automated systems, on the other hand, follow predefined protocols and processes, ensuring that every step is executed consistently and accurately. This minimizes the risk of errors, increases efficiency, and allows IT teams to focus on resolving the root causes of patch issues, rather than spending time on the manual aspects of the recovery process.

As organizations continue to rely more heavily on their IT infrastructure to support day-to-day operations, the need for robust and efficient patch management systems becomes even more critical. Automating patch rollbacks and recovery processes is an essential strategy for minimizing downtime and maintaining business continuity. By integrating real-time monitoring, version control, backup systems, and AI-driven predictive capabilities, organizations can ensure that their systems are quickly restored to a stable state following a patch failure. This proactive approach not only helps to protect sensitive data and maintain operational efficiency but also provides peace of mind, knowing that automated processes are in place to handle unexpected issues swiftly and effectively.

Understanding the Role of Zero-Day Exploits in Patch Management

Zero-day exploits represent one of the most significant threats in cybersecurity today. These exploits target vulnerabilities in software or hardware that are unknown to the vendor or the public, and for which no patch exists at the time of the attack. A zero-day exploit is so named because once the vulnerability is discovered, the vendor has zero days to create and release a patch before the vulnerability can be exploited. For organizations, this creates a serious challenge, particularly when it comes to patch management. The presence of zero-day vulnerabilities can leave systems exposed to attacks, sometimes for extended periods, until a patch or fix is developed. In this context, patch management becomes not just about deploying patches but also about staying proactive and responsive to the potential threats posed by these unknown vulnerabilities.

The existence of zero-day exploits complicates patch management because organizations are left in a reactive position. Vendors typically release patches in response to vulnerabilities that have been discovered, often after the fact. In the case of zero-day vulnerabilities, no patch is initially available, leaving systems at risk. The danger of zero-day exploits lies in the fact that cybercriminals are often able to exploit these vulnerabilities before they are discovered and patched by the vendor. Attackers can leverage zero-day vulnerabilities to compromise sensitive data, execute malicious code, or cause widespread disruption to organizational operations. The difficulty for IT teams and organizations is that they cannot defend against an exploit for which no patch exists. This dynamic places even greater emphasis on proactive security measures, including network monitoring, threat intelligence, and behavioral analysis, to detect potential zero-day attacks early on.

Zero-day exploits also have a high level of sophistication, making them particularly dangerous. Often, attackers will use zero-day vulnerabilities to develop malware that is hard to detect and even harder to defend against. For example, a zero-day exploit may be used to install a backdoor, allowing the attacker continuous access to the compromised system. Since the vulnerability is unknown to the vendor, traditional security tools like antivirus software or firewalls may fail to detect the exploit. This makes it more challenging for organizations to prevent attacks based solely on known signatures or patterns. As such, organizations must incorporate advanced security measures to detect anomalies or suspicious behavior that may indicate a zero-day attack is underway.

Given the nature of zero-day exploits, patch management plays a pivotal role in mitigating their risks. Once a vulnerability is discovered and a patch is developed, it is critical for organizations to implement the patch as soon as possible. However, the challenge is that organizations may not always be aware of a zero-day vulnerability until it is actively being exploited in the wild. In some cases, zero-day exploits are discovered through targeted attacks or as part of a broader cybersecurity research initiative. Once a patch is made available, organizations need to quickly deploy it to ensure that their systems are protected from any potential attacks. This highlights the importance of having a well-organized and responsive patch management system that can rapidly identify and apply patches for vulnerabilities once they are disclosed.

Because zero-day exploits are typically discovered after an attack has occurred, organizations must be agile in their patch management practices. They need to be prepared to react quickly and effectively to the release of patches for zero-day vulnerabilities. Effective patch management systems must incorporate automation to ensure that patches can be deployed quickly and accurately across the network. Automated patching tools can scan systems, identify missing patches, and deploy updates across the infrastructure with minimal downtime. This is particularly important in environments where systems are spread across multiple locations or where time-sensitive data is being processed. The ability to quickly patch vulnerable systems helps to reduce the window of opportunity for attackers to exploit zero-day vulnerabilities and significantly mitigates the risk of data breaches or other security incidents.

In addition to the technical aspects of patch management, organizations must also focus on maintaining a comprehensive and proactive security strategy to address zero-day vulnerabilities. While patching is an essential defense, it should not be the only line of defense. Regular vulnerability assessments, penetration testing, and network monitoring are critical components of a broader security strategy aimed at identifying potential threats, including zero-day vulnerabilities. Vulnerability assessments help organizations understand their risk profile and identify weaknesses in their systems that could potentially be exploited. Penetration testing, where ethical hackers simulate real-world attacks, helps organizations evaluate their defenses against advanced threats, including zero-day exploits. These proactive measures, combined with a responsive patch management process, allow organizations to better prepare for and respond to zero-day vulnerabilities.

Threat intelligence is also an important tool in addressing the risks posed by zero-day exploits. By subscribing to threat intelligence feeds or participating in information-sharing initiatives, organizations can gain early insights into potential zero-day threats and vulnerabilities. This allows them to prepare and implement mitigations before a zero-day exploit is actively used in an attack. Additionally, threat intelligence can help organizations identify emerging vulnerabilities that may not yet have patches available, giving them time to implement temporary defenses, such as network segmentation or behavior-based detection systems, to protect against attacks targeting those vulnerabilities.

Furthermore, communication is an essential component of patch management in the context of zero-day exploits. As vulnerabilities are discovered and patches are released, it is critical for vendors, security teams, and organizations to maintain open lines of communication. Vendors must notify customers as soon as possible about the availability of patches for zero-day vulnerabilities, while organizations must communicate internally to ensure that patching efforts are coordinated across departments and business units. External communication is also important, as organizations may need to inform stakeholders, clients, or customers about potential security risks and the steps they are taking to mitigate them. This transparency builds trust and ensures that all parties are aware of the efforts being made to address vulnerabilities and protect sensitive information.

The threat of zero-day exploits underscores the importance of having a proactive, multi-layered security strategy that incorporates timely patch management practices. The rapid discovery and deployment of patches for zero-day vulnerabilities are essential to reducing the risk of exploitation, but organizations must also implement additional security measures, such as behavioral analysis, threat intelligence, and vulnerability scanning, to detect and mitigate attacks before they cause significant harm. Furthermore, organizations must be agile, ensuring that their patch management processes are flexible enough to address emerging vulnerabilities swiftly and effectively. By combining proactive security practices with a streamlined and automated patch management system, organizations can better defend against the ever-evolving threats posed by zero-day exploits, reducing their exposure to attacks and enhancing their overall security posture.

Integrating Patch Management with Vulnerability Management Programs

Patch management and vulnerability management are two essential components of an organization's cybersecurity strategy, but they are often treated as separate processes. However, when integrated effectively, they form a powerful defense against security breaches and help ensure that an organization's IT infrastructure remains secure, up-to-date, and resilient against evolving threats. Integrating patch management with vulnerability management allows for a more coordinated, proactive approach to identifying, assessing, and addressing vulnerabilities, ultimately improving the overall security posture of the organization.

At its core, vulnerability management involves identifying, evaluating, and prioritizing vulnerabilities within an organization's IT infrastructure. This process begins with scanning systems, applications, and network devices to identify known vulnerabilities, often using vulnerability scanning tools and threat intelligence feeds. Once vulnerabilities are identified, they are assessed to determine their severity, the potential impact on the organization, and the likelihood of exploitation. From there, a risk-based approach is taken to prioritize which vulnerabilities should be addressed first. Patch management, on the other hand, is the process of applying updates and patches to systems to address these vulnerabilities. Patches are typically released by software vendors to fix security holes, improve performance, or add new features. When these two processes are integrated, the organization can ensure that vulnerabilities are not only identified but are also effectively mitigated through timely patching.

One of the main benefits of integrating patch management with vulnerability management is the ability to streamline the process of identifying and remediating vulnerabilities. Without integration, organizations may identify vulnerabilities through regular vulnerability scans but may fail to apply patches in a timely manner, leaving systems exposed to potential attacks. By integrating patch management into the vulnerability management process, vulnerabilities can be addressed more quickly, as patching becomes an automatic response to identified threats. When a vulnerability is discovered and prioritized, patching can be scheduled and deployed as part of the remediation process, reducing the time between identification and mitigation. This integrated approach helps organizations minimize the window of opportunity for attackers to exploit vulnerabilities, thereby reducing the risk of a breach or attack.

Additionally, integrating patch management with vulnerability management enables organizations to prioritize patching efforts more effectively. Not all vulnerabilities carry the same level of risk, and applying patches indiscriminately to all systems without considering the severity of the vulnerabilities can be inefficient and disruptive. Vulnerability management tools provide valuable insight into which vulnerabilities pose the greatest risk to the organization based on factors such as the vulnerability's CVSS (Common Vulnerability Scoring System) score, the system's exposure to external threats, and the criticality of the affected system. By integrating patch management into the vulnerability management process, organizations can ensure that patches are deployed first to the most critical systems and those with the highest risk. This targeted approach helps to optimize the use of resources, ensuring that the most impactful vulnerabilities are addressed first.

Another advantage of this integration is the ability to automate and simplify the entire patching process. In traditional patch management, administrators must manually track patches, monitor updates, and deploy them across various systems. This manual process can be time-consuming and prone to error, especially in large, complex IT environments. By integrating patch management with vulnerability management tools, organizations can automate many aspects of the patching process. Vulnerability management tools can automatically identify missing patches and provide administrators with a centralized view of which systems are up-to-date and which need updates. These tools can also schedule and deploy patches automatically, ensuring that systems are patched in a timely manner without requiring significant manual intervention. Automation not only reduces the burden on IT staff but also helps to ensure that patches are applied consistently across the organization.

The integration of patch management and vulnerability management also facilitates continuous monitoring and reporting. Vulnerability management tools typically include features that allow organizations to track the status of vulnerabilities over time. When patch management is integrated, this monitoring extends to the patch deployment process. Organizations can track which patches have been applied, identify any systems that are still missing patches, and assess the effectiveness of their patching efforts. Regular reports can be generated to provide a clear picture of the organization's patching status and overall security posture. This visibility is essential for maintaining compliance with regulatory standards and for providing management with the information needed to make informed decisions about security priorities and resource allocation.

Furthermore, integrating patch management with vulnerability management helps organizations stay ahead of emerging threats. Vulnerabilities are constantly being discovered, and cybercriminals are quick to exploit newly identified security holes. A coordinated approach allows organizations to remain proactive in addressing these threats. As new vulnerabilities are discovered, vulnerability management tools provide real-time information about these threats, including any available patches or fixes. By incorporating patch management into this process, organizations can respond quickly to newly identified vulnerabilities, applying patches as soon as they are released and ensuring that their systems remain protected against the latest threats. This proactive response is particularly important in industries where security breaches can have severe consequences, such as healthcare, finance, and government.

A critical part of the integration process is the feedback loop between vulnerability assessment and patch effectiveness. Vulnerability management involves scanning and assessing the security posture of systems regularly, but to ensure that a patch has been effective, follow-up scans and validation processes are necessary. After deploying a patch, organizations should re-scan the affected systems to ensure that the vulnerability has been remediated and that no new vulnerabilities have been introduced. This validation step is essential in ensuring that patching efforts are successful and that vulnerabilities have been fully mitigated. Integration ensures that vulnerability management and patch management are closely linked, allowing for continuous validation and assessment of patch effectiveness.

Integrating patch management with vulnerability management also enhances an organization's ability to respond to incidents more efficiently. When a security breach occurs, the organization can quickly determine whether the attack exploited a known vulnerability. If a patch for the vulnerability exists, the integration allows for a quick response in deploying the necessary fix to affected systems, helping to contain the damage and reduce recovery time. Moreover, this integrated approach enables organizations to prioritize patching efforts during a security incident based on the severity of the vulnerability being exploited, ensuring that the most critical vulnerabilities are addressed first.

For smaller organizations or those with limited IT resources, integrating patch management with vulnerability management tools can significantly improve the efficiency and effectiveness of their security efforts. By automating vulnerability scanning, patch detection, and deployment, even organizations with smaller IT teams can keep their systems secure and compliant with regulatory standards. Additionally, this integration allows organizations to maximize the value of their security investments, ensuring that patches are applied quickly and vulnerabilities are addressed in a timely manner.

The integration of patch management with vulnerability management is essential for organizations seeking to stay secure in the face of rapidly evolving cyber threats. By combining the proactive identification of vulnerabilities with the timely deployment of patches, organizations can reduce their exposure to risks, optimize their security resources, and maintain the integrity of their IT systems. This coordinated approach to vulnerability and patch management ensures that security efforts are streamlined, efficient, and capable of responding quickly to emerging threats. Through integration, organizations can create a more resilient security posture, reducing the chances of successful cyberattacks and minimizing the impact of any incidents that do occur.

Managing Patches in a Remote or Distributed Workforce

The rapid shift towards remote and distributed workforces has introduced new complexities for IT teams responsible for managing and securing organizational systems. The traditional model of patch management, where updates are applied to systems within a centralized network, has evolved. With employees working from home or across various remote locations, maintaining consistent and timely patching of devices has become more challenging. Despite these challenges, patch management remains a critical aspect of maintaining security, ensuring compliance, and preventing vulnerabilities in a distributed workforce environment. Effectively managing patches for remote or distributed workers requires organizations to adapt their strategies, tools, and processes to ensure that all devices, regardless of their location, remain up-to-date and secure.

In a traditional office setup, systems are often physically accessible to IT staff, making patch deployment and verification relatively straightforward. However, with remote and distributed workforces, the devices that require patching are spread out across multiple locations, which can significantly complicate the process. Devices may be located in employees' homes or other remote locations, and IT teams often lack the physical access to directly interact with those systems. This means that organizations need to implement remote patch management solutions that can effectively deploy patches to employees' devices regardless of where they are located. The absence of physical proximity demands a shift to more automated and remote patch management practices that rely on cloud-based tools and centralized management systems.

One of the key challenges of managing patches for a remote workforce is ensuring that all devices are consistently updated. With employees using a wide variety of devices, from laptops and desktops to mobile phones and tablets, the need for a unified patching system that works across all platforms is critical. Patch management tools that support cross-platform compatibility are essential in a remote work environment. These tools allow IT teams to deploy patches to a diverse array of devices, ensuring that no system is left unpatched, regardless of its operating system or device type. Automated patching tools, which can remotely push updates to all systems without requiring manual intervention, are particularly valuable in ensuring that all devices are up to date with the latest security patches and software updates.

Additionally, managing patches for a remote workforce involves handling the security concerns associated with varying network environments. In an office setting, systems are typically connected to a secure, controlled network, making it easier for IT teams to monitor and manage devices. However, remote workers are often connecting to the internet via home networks, public Wi-Fi, or other less-secure environments. This introduces additional risks, as systems may be vulnerable to attacks if the security measures in place at the employee's home network are insufficient. IT teams must ensure that patches are deployed in a way that accounts for these risks, leveraging secure channels for patch distribution and making sure that systems are updated without exposing sensitive data. Encryption, secure VPN connections, and multi-factor authentication are some of the tools that can be used to bolster security and protect patching processes during remote deployments.

Another challenge in managing patches for a distributed workforce is ensuring compliance with patching schedules and maintaining documentation of patching activities. Many industries require organizations to comply with specific regulations regarding the timely application of security patches. In a remote work environment, it can be difficult to track which devices have been patched and which still require updates. Centralized patch management platforms that allow IT teams to monitor the patching status of all devices in real-time are essential for ensuring compliance. These platforms provide visibility into the entire organization's patch management efforts, helping to identify systems that are out of date or vulnerable to known security threats. Automated reporting features within these platforms can also generate compliance reports, allowing organizations to demonstrate that they are meeting regulatory requirements for patching and update management.

The complexity of patch management in a remote or distributed workforce is further heightened by the potential for employees to delay or ignore patching notifications. In a traditional office environment, IT teams can directly oversee patching activities, ensuring that devices are updated in a timely manner. However, with remote workers, it can be difficult to enforce compliance. Employees may ignore update notifications, defer patches to avoid downtime, or simply forget to apply them altogether. To address this, organizations should implement user education and training programs to highlight the importance of patching and its role in protecting both personal and organizational data. Regular reminders, as well as a clear communication strategy, can help reinforce the message that patching is not just an IT responsibility but a shared duty to protect the organization's security. Additionally, incentives or enforced policies that require updates to be applied within a specific timeframe can help improve adherence to patching schedules.

Effective patch management also requires IT teams to test patches before deployment to ensure that they do not cause issues or disruptions to employee workflows. Remote workers may rely on systems and applications that are critical to their job functions, and untested patches can lead to system crashes or application malfunctions, which can be disruptive and detrimental to productivity. To avoid these issues, patches should be thoroughly tested in a controlled environment before being pushed out to remote devices. Automated patch management solutions often include testing and validation features that allow patches to be deployed first to a small group of users or systems to assess their impact. This approach minimizes the risk of widespread issues and ensures that the patching process does not disrupt business operations.

A crucial component of managing patches for a remote workforce is ensuring that patch management systems are scalable and flexible. As organizations grow and remote work becomes more common, the number of devices needing patches will likely increase. A scalable patch management solution allows organizations to accommodate this growth, deploying patches across an expanding workforce without sacrificing efficiency or security. These systems should be able to handle a wide range of devices, from employee laptops and desktop systems to mobile phones, ensuring that every device is kept secure and up to date, regardless of location.

In addition to the technical aspects, effective patch management in remote work environments also requires collaboration and communication between IT teams and remote employees. IT teams must work closely with employees to ensure that patches are deployed in a way that minimizes disruption. Clear communication regarding scheduled patch deployments, expected downtime, and the importance of applying patches in a timely manner helps to ensure that remote workers are prepared for updates and understand their role in keeping systems secure. Additionally, IT teams should provide remote employees with support channels to address any issues or questions that arise during or after the patching process.

Ultimately, managing patches in a remote or distributed workforce requires a combination of the right technology, processes, and communication. By implementing automated patch management solutions, ensuring compliance with patching schedules, securing remote connections, and providing employee training, organizations can effectively manage their patching efforts in a distributed work environment. This proactive approach helps to ensure that systems remain secure, employees remain productive, and organizations can continue to operate smoothly without compromising their security posture. Patch management for remote workers is an ongoing effort, but with the right tools and strategies, organizations can minimize the risks associated with outdated systems and ensure a secure, resilient infrastructure.

Leveraging Artificial Intelligence for Patch Management Efficiency

As organizations face increasing cyber threats and a growing number of vulnerabilities within their IT systems, efficient patch management has become a cornerstone of an effective cybersecurity strategy. However, traditional patch management processes can be time-consuming, error-prone, and resource-intensive, particularly in large or complex environments. This is where artificial intelligence (AI) can play a transformative role, enhancing the speed, accuracy, and scalability of patch management. By integrating AI into patch management processes, organizations can streamline operations, reduce risks associated with vulnerabilities, and improve overall security posture.

AI can significantly improve patch management by automating several aspects of the process. Traditionally, patch management has involved manual tasks, such as identifying vulnerabilities, tracking patches, testing patches, and deploying them across systems. AI-powered systems, on the other hand, can automate these tasks, reducing the burden on IT teams and ensuring that patches are deployed faster and more consistently. For example, AI-driven patch management tools can continuously scan systems for missing patches, using machine learning algorithms to identify vulnerabilities and recommend appropriate patches. These systems can also prioritize patches based on the severity of the vulnerabilities they address, ensuring that the most critical patches are applied first. This automation not only saves time but also improves the accuracy of patching, minimizing the risk of human error.

One of the key benefits of AI in patch management is its ability to predict and prevent issues before they occur. Machine learning algorithms can analyze historical data and patterns to predict which systems are most likely to be vulnerable to future attacks or which patches are most likely to cause problems during deployment. This predictive capability allows IT teams to proactively address potential issues before they escalate, reducing the likelihood of system downtime or security breaches. By analyzing trends in patching failures or the success rates of different patches, AI can identify the most effective approaches to patch deployment, optimizing the overall process.

Furthermore, AI can enhance the testing phase of patch management, which is often one of the most time-consuming and critical aspects of the process. Before deploying patches across an organization's systems, IT teams typically test them in controlled environments to ensure that they do not cause disruptions or compatibility issues. AI can expedite this process by automatically simulating the patch deployment on a range of systems and configurations. Using AI-driven testing platforms, organizations can quickly identify potential conflicts, incompatibilities, or performance issues that could arise from applying a particular patch. These platforms can also assess the effectiveness of patches by simulating real-world scenarios in which vulnerabilities might be exploited. This reduces the need for manual testing and ensures that patches are more thoroughly vetted before deployment.

In addition to testing, AI can streamline the patch deployment phase itself. Deploying patches to a large number of systems, particularly in a diverse IT environment, can be a daunting task. AI-based patch management tools can automatically deploy patches across different systems, ensuring that updates are applied consistently and promptly. These tools can schedule patch deployment during off-peak hours to minimize disruptions, automatically roll back patches if issues arise, and provide real-time monitoring of the deployment process. AI can also adapt to the unique needs of an organization's infrastructure, ensuring that patches are applied based on specific criteria such as system type, vulnerability severity, and business priorities. This level of customization and automation ensures that patches are deployed efficiently and without unnecessary delays.

Another significant advantage of leveraging AI in patch management is the ability to continuously monitor and improve the process. AI-powered systems can track patch deployment over time, identifying patterns in patching success and failure. By collecting and analyzing data from past patch deployments, these systems can generate insights into which patches were most effective, which systems experienced the most issues, and where improvements can be made in future deployments. This continuous learning process allows organizations to fine-tune their patch management strategies, improving both efficiency and security over time. AI can also help with reporting and compliance, automatically generating reports on patch deployment status, success rates, and the security posture of systems, making it easier for organizations to meet regulatory requirements.

AI's role in patch management extends beyond simply automating routine tasks—it can also help organizations stay ahead of emerging threats. As vulnerabilities are discovered, AI can be used to identify new threats and assess their potential impact on the organization's systems. For example, AI-powered threat intelligence tools can analyze security advisories and research papers, automatically flagging new vulnerabilities that may require patches. AI can also track the exploits of these vulnerabilities in the wild, helping IT teams understand the urgency of deploying specific patches. By integrating AI with threat intelligence, organizations can ensure that their patch management strategies are aligned with the latest security risks, allowing them to respond quickly and effectively to new threats.

In addition to improving the technical aspects of patch management, AI can also enhance communication and collaboration within an organization. As patch management becomes more automated, IT teams can focus on higher-level tasks, such as strategy development, risk management, and coordination with other departments. AI-powered systems can provide real-time alerts and notifications to relevant stakeholders, ensuring that decision-makers are always informed about the status of patching efforts. For example, AI can notify IT managers when critical patches are deployed or when patches fail to install, allowing them to take immediate action. This improved communication ensures that all team members are aligned and that potential issues are addressed quickly.

While the benefits of AI in patch management are clear, it is important to recognize that implementing AI solutions requires careful planning and consideration. Organizations must assess their current patch management processes and determine where AI can provide the most value. This may involve selecting the right AI-driven tools, integrating them with existing systems, and training IT teams to work with new technologies. Organizations should also ensure that AI-based solutions are regularly updated and refined to keep pace with evolving threats and vulnerabilities. Finally, organizations must strike a balance between automation and human oversight, ensuring that AI enhances—not replaces—the expertise and judgment of IT professionals.

The integration of AI into patch management has the potential to revolutionize the way organizations manage security vulnerabilities and system updates. By automating routine tasks, predicting future risks, optimizing patch deployment, and continuously improving processes, AI can help organizations maintain secure, efficient, and resilient IT infrastructures. With the growing complexity of IT environments and the increasing sophistication of cyber threats, leveraging AI for patch management is no longer just a competitive advantage; it has become a necessity for organizations striving to stay ahead in the digital age.

The Security Implications of Postponing Patch Deployments

In the world of cybersecurity, patch management plays a critical role in protecting systems from vulnerabilities and ensuring the continued integrity of an organization's infrastructure. Patches are often released to fix bugs, improve functionality, and, most importantly, address security vulnerabilities that could be exploited by attackers. However, despite the importance of patching, many organizations postpone or delay deploying patches for a variety of reasons. While this delay may seem like a minor issue in the short term, the security implications of postponing patch deployments can be severe and far-reaching. The longer patches are delayed, the greater the risk that an attacker will exploit the vulnerabilities they address, leading to potential breaches, data loss, financial damage, and long-term reputational harm.

One of the most significant security risks associated with postponing patch deployments is the increased exposure to known vulnerabilities. When a patch is released, it typically addresses a vulnerability that has been identified in a system, software, or application. These vulnerabilities, once known, are often targeted by cybercriminals who can use them to gain unauthorized access, escalate privileges, or execute malicious code. Postponing the deployment of a patch means that an organization's systems remain vulnerable for longer, providing attackers with a wider window of opportunity to exploit the weakness. This delay in patching increases the likelihood that attackers will successfully breach the system, compromise sensitive data, or deploy malware that can cause significant damage.

The risk of a security breach is especially high when patches address vulnerabilities in widely used software or systems. Attackers are keenly aware of these common vulnerabilities and often use automated tools to scan networks for unpatched systems. Once they identify a vulnerable system, they can exploit the weakness and gain access to the organization's network. Popular software, operating systems, and applications are often primary targets for cybercriminals because they are used by so many organizations, making them high-value targets. Delaying patch deployment in these instances can have catastrophic consequences, as it essentially gives attackers a green light to exploit the vulnerability and launch an attack.

Another critical issue that arises from delaying patches is the potential for ransomware attacks. Ransomware is a form of malicious software that encrypts a victim's data and demands a ransom in exchange for the decryption key. Many ransomware attacks are successful because attackers exploit known vulnerabilities in systems that have not been patched. Postponing patch deployments can give ransomware operators the time they need to launch their attacks, particularly if the vulnerability being exploited is one that has already been publicly disclosed. Once ransomware gains access to the network, it can quickly spread, encrypting critical data and crippling business operations. The financial impact of such attacks can be severe, especially for small and medium-sized enterprises (SMEs), which may struggle to recover from the costs of paying the ransom, restoring systems, and addressing reputational damage.

The security implications of postponed patch deployments also extend to compliance risks. Many industries, including healthcare, finance, and retail, are subject to strict regulations and standards regarding data protection and cybersecurity. These regulations often include specific requirements for patch management, mandating that organizations apply security patches in a timely manner. Delaying patch deployments can result in non-compliance with these regulations, exposing organizations to potential fines, legal penalties, and loss of business licenses. Additionally, if a breach occurs as a result of delayed patching, organizations may be found liable for failing to meet regulatory requirements, leading to further legal and financial consequences. Non-compliance due to postponed patching can also undermine customer trust, as clients expect organizations to prioritize the security of their data and adhere to industry best practices.

Furthermore, the consequences of postponing patches can affect the broader security ecosystem. Cybercriminals are constantly evolving their tactics and developing new techniques to exploit vulnerabilities. When an organization delays patch deployment, it contributes to the larger problem of unpatched systems across the internet. This not only puts the organization at risk but also encourages the spread of malicious activity. Cybercriminals often target organizations that have failed to patch their systems, knowing that these systems are easier to compromise. As one organization becomes a victim of a breach due to delayed patching, it can lead to a chain reaction, with other organizations being targeted through similar vulnerabilities. In this way, a failure to deploy patches promptly does not just put one organization at risk but can have far-reaching consequences across industries and sectors.

In some cases, delayed patching can also cause system instability and performance issues. While patches are typically designed to address security vulnerabilities, they can also fix bugs or improve the overall functionality of a system. When patches are delayed, systems may continue to operate with known issues that can lead to reduced performance, crashes, or unexpected behavior. These issues may not always be immediately apparent but can affect the user experience, reduce productivity, and even cause data corruption or loss. The longer a patch is postponed, the greater the likelihood that other issues will arise, compounding the risk and leading to more severe problems down the road.

Another security implication of delayed patch deployments is the potential for a delay in responding to emerging threats. The cybersecurity landscape is constantly evolving, with new threats and vulnerabilities emerging regularly. Patches are often released not just to address known vulnerabilities, but to protect systems from newly discovered threats. By postponing patches, organizations are not only leaving themselves exposed to vulnerabilities that have been identified, but they are also increasing the risk of being blindsided by new and emerging threats. Attackers can take advantage of the delay, deploying new exploits or attack vectors that are specifically designed to target unpatched systems. This delay in patching leaves organizations less equipped to respond to the rapidly changing threat environment, putting them at a significant disadvantage.

The longer patches are postponed, the more expensive and complicated it becomes to address the vulnerabilities later. Initially, patching may seem like a minor task that can be deferred, especially if the patch does not appear to be urgent. However, over time, the impact of these unpatched vulnerabilities accumulates. The cost of remediating a breach or recovering from an attack is often far greater than the cost of simply applying a patch in a timely manner. Additionally, the longer an organization waits to patch, the more likely it is that systems will become misaligned, requiring complex and time-consuming efforts to update multiple systems at once.

The security implications of postponing patch deployments are profound and multifaceted. By delaying patches, organizations expose themselves to the risk of cyberattacks, compliance failures, reputational damage, and operational disruptions. The consequences of such delays can be severe, affecting not only the organization's security but also its ability to function and maintain customer trust. To minimize these risks, organizations must prioritize timely patching, automate the process where possible, and continuously assess the risks associated with delayed updates. Addressing patch management in a timely and efficient manner is essential to maintaining a secure and resilient IT infrastructure.

Patch Management for Mobile Devices and Operating Systems

In today's fast-paced digital world, mobile devices have become indispensable tools for both personal and professional use. From smartphones and tablets to laptops and other mobile computing devices, these tools allow users to stay connected, access information, and perform critical business functions on the go. As mobile devices become more integrated into organizational workflows, maintaining their security becomes increasingly important. One of the most vital aspects of securing mobile devices is patch management, which ensures that operating systems and applications remain up to date with the latest security fixes and functionality improvements. Patch management for mobile devices and operating systems presents unique challenges compared to traditional desktop or server systems, but it is essential for minimizing vulnerabilities and protecting sensitive data in a mobile-first world.

Mobile devices are inherently different from desktop systems in several ways, making patch management more complex. One of the biggest challenges in managing patches for mobile devices is the diversity of operating systems and hardware. While desktop systems typically run a limited number of operating systems (such as Windows, macOS, or Linux), mobile devices are more varied. The two dominant mobile operating systems are Apple's iOS and Google's Android, each with its own set of patching requirements, release cycles, and user interfaces. Additionally, mobile devices come in a wide variety of models from different manufacturers, each with its own customizations and hardware specifications. This fragmentation makes it more difficult to develop a uniform patch management strategy, as patches for one device or operating system may not be applicable to another.

Another challenge with mobile patch management is the role of app stores and third-party apps in the patching process. On traditional desktops, software vendors typically control the distribution of patches, but on mobile devices, applications are distributed through third-party app stores such as Apple's App Store and Google Play. While these app stores have strict guidelines for application security, mobile applications often require independent updates to fix

127

vulnerabilities, which may not always align with the mobile operating system's patching schedule. As a result, patching mobile apps requires coordination between operating system updates and third-party application updates. Mobile devices are often more exposed to security risks because many users fail to update their applications in a timely manner, either because they are unaware of the updates or because the process is too cumbersome.

Managing patch deployments on mobile devices also presents logistical challenges due to the widespread use of Bring Your Own Device (BYOD) policies in many organizations. In a BYOD environment, employees use their personal mobile devices to access corporate resources, such as email, cloud applications, and internal databases. These devices may not be under the same strict management controls as corporate-owned devices, making it difficult for IT teams to ensure that patches are applied consistently and on time. Mobile devices in a BYOD setup may have varying levels of software and security configurations, and employees may disable automatic updates or delay updates due to concerns about performance or the need to maintain a device's battery life. This creates a gap in security, as unpatched devices remain vulnerable to exploitation.

Another key concern in mobile patch management is the rapid pace of software updates and the short lifespan of mobile devices. Operating system vendors, particularly Apple and Google, release regular updates to address security vulnerabilities and introduce new features. These updates must be applied promptly to mitigate security risks. However, the rapid pace at which these updates are released can create a backlog for IT teams, especially when devices are spread across various geographic locations or managed by different users. Additionally, older devices or devices running outdated operating system versions may not be eligible for new updates, which creates a critical issue in maintaining device security. In many cases, mobile operating system vendors stop supporting older models after a certain period, leaving these devices vulnerable to exploitation if they cannot be upgraded to newer versions.

The mobile environment also introduces risks related to data protection. Mobile devices are often used in public or unsecured networks, such as Wi-Fi in cafes or airports, where data is more susceptible to interception. As these devices are often used to access sensitive corporate data, unpatched systems can provide a backdoor for attackers to intercept communication or steal information. With the rise of mobile banking, online shopping, and other financial transactions on mobile devices, unpatched vulnerabilities can lead to unauthorized access to sensitive personal and financial data. Effective patch management ensures that these vulnerabilities are addressed, reducing the risk of data breaches, identity theft, and other malicious activities.

To address these challenges, organizations need a comprehensive approach to mobile patch management that involves both proactive and reactive strategies. Proactively, businesses should implement mobile device management (MDM) solutions that allow IT teams to monitor, manage, and enforce security policies on mobile devices. MDM tools can ensure that devices are enrolled in automatic patching systems, which can push updates and patches to devices as soon as they are released. These tools also help IT teams track patch deployment progress, identify unpatched devices, and remotely wipe devices if they become compromised or are lost.

Another important strategy for effective mobile patch management is user education. Many mobile security issues arise from user behavior, such as failing to apply updates or downloading apps from untrusted sources. Organizations should regularly educate employees about the importance of patching their devices and ensure they understand the security risks associated with delayed updates. Additionally, businesses can implement policies that require employees to keep their devices updated as part of the organization's security protocol, with consequences for non-compliance.

In addition to enforcing patch deployment, organizations must consider the compatibility of patches with mobile applications. Mobile device operating systems are tightly integrated with the apps running on them, and a single patch to the operating system can have a significant impact on app functionality. When deploying patches, IT teams must ensure that the updates do not disrupt business-critical applications or interfere with user productivity. This requires a combination of rigorous testing and collaboration with app developers to verify that patches do not introduce new issues. Ideally, IT teams should test patches in a controlled environment before wide deployment to ensure they do not break existing workflows or lead to application crashes.

Automation also plays a crucial role in mobile patch management. Many mobile devices can be configured to receive automatic updates for both operating systems and applications, reducing the burden on employees to manually apply patches. Automation helps ensure that patches are applied promptly and consistently, without requiring manual intervention. Automated patch management systems can also reduce human error, ensuring that no devices are overlooked and that critical security vulnerabilities are addressed without delay.

The importance of maintaining mobile device security cannot be overstated, particularly as mobile devices become more integrated into the fabric of organizational operations. The security of mobile devices is directly tied to an organization's ability to maintain a proactive patch management strategy. By using tools such as MDM solutions, enforcing strict update policies, educating users, and automating patch deployments, organizations can ensure that mobile devices remain secure, compliant, and resilient against evolving threats. Given the rapid pace of mobile technology and the increasing sophistication of cyber threats, maintaining effective patch management for mobile devices is essential for safeguarding sensitive data and maintaining business continuity in a mobile-first world.

Evaluating the Risks of Patch Failures and Breakages

In the realm of IT security, patch management is an essential process for maintaining system integrity, addressing vulnerabilities, and preventing cyberattacks. However, patching, while necessary, is not without its risks. Patches, though designed to fix vulnerabilities and improve system functionality, can occasionally introduce new issues, break existing functionality, or cause system failures. Patch failures and breakages represent a significant concern for IT administrators, as these issues can lead to system downtime, productivity loss, and, in the worst cases, security vulnerabilities. Evaluating the risks associated with patch failures and breakages is crucial for organizations to mitigate potential damage and ensure that their patch management processes do not inadvertently compromise the systems they are meant to protect.

When a patch is deployed, its primary goal is to address security vulnerabilities, fix bugs, or enhance system performance. In an ideal world, patches would deploy seamlessly and have no unintended side effects. Unfortunately, the reality is that patches may fail to apply correctly, causing systems to behave unpredictably or, in some cases, become completely unusable. Patch failures can occur for a variety of reasons, such as compatibility issues with existing software, insufficient system resources, or errors in the patching process itself. The severity of the failure can vary, from minor bugs or performance degradation to complete system crashes. In either case, patch failures undermine the purpose of the patching process, leaving systems exposed to vulnerabilities or causing operational disruptions.

One of the key risks of patch failures is the potential for system downtime. For organizations that rely heavily on their IT infrastructure for daily operations, even short periods of downtime can have significant consequences. Systems that fail to update properly may require extensive troubleshooting to identify the root cause of the issue, and the time required to resolve these problems can impact productivity, revenue, and customer satisfaction. In mission-critical environments, such as healthcare or finance, where systems need to be operational around the clock, the consequences of patch failures can be even more severe. The impact of downtime extends beyond immediate operational disruption, as it can affect business continuity, lead to service interruptions, and damage an organization's reputation.

Another significant risk of patch failures is the potential introduction of new security vulnerabilities. While patches are meant to close existing security holes, a failure to apply them correctly can leave systems even more exposed to threats. In some cases, patches may inadvertently create new vulnerabilities or fail to address the underlying issue they were intended to fix. For example, a patch that addresses one security flaw may inadvertently conflict with another part of the system, opening up a new avenue for exploitation. Additionally, a patch that breaks functionality may prevent other security measures from operating correctly, leaving systems vulnerable to attack. In this scenario, rather than strengthening security, the patch failure may inadvertently give attackers the opportunity to exploit new weaknesses that would not have been present if the patch had been applied successfully.

Patch breakages can also lead to performance issues, further complicating system management. While some patches may fail outright, others may apply but result in performance degradation. After a patch is deployed, systems may experience slower processing times, increased resource consumption, or erratic behavior. These performance issues can be particularly problematic in large-scale environments, where multiple systems are interconnected and depend on one another. Performance problems resulting from patch failures can ripple through an entire network, causing cascading issues that affect multiple systems and workflows. As a result, IT teams may find themselves addressing performance bottlenecks and resource allocation problems, in addition to dealing with the underlying causes of the patch failure.

The complexity of modern IT infrastructures compounds the risks associated with patch failures. Today's networks often consist of a mix of on-premises systems, cloud-based services, and hybrid environments that all need to be patched and maintained regularly. When a patch fails to deploy on one system, it can create compatibility issues with other systems that rely on the same or related software. In environments that use a wide variety of applications, operating systems, and configurations, a patch failure can trigger a cascade of issues that affect other systems in the network. This interdependency can make troubleshooting patch failures a time-consuming and difficult process, especially if the failure is not immediately apparent. The complexity of these systems increases the likelihood that patch failures will go unnoticed for some time, leaving the organization exposed to both technical and security risks.

Evaluating the risks associated with patch failures and breakages also requires an understanding of the potential long-term impact on an organization's security posture. When patches fail, vulnerabilities remain unaddressed, and security gaps persist. Attackers are constantly looking for opportunities to exploit these gaps, and a failure to apply a critical patch can leave an organization vulnerable to a cyberattack. This is especially concerning in the context of zero-day exploits, where attackers may target newly discovered vulnerabilities that have not yet been patched. Even if patches are eventually applied, the delay in patching creates a window of opportunity for attackers to exploit the vulnerability before it is fixed. In this sense, patch failures not only impact immediate operations but can also have long-lasting security implications.

One of the most challenging aspects of patch failure management is the need for a comprehensive testing and validation process. To minimize the risks of patch failures, organizations must ensure that patches are thoroughly tested before deployment. In complex IT environments, testing patches in a controlled setting is essential for identifying potential issues before they affect production systems. However, testing patches is not always a foolproof process, as new compatibility problems may only arise after the patch is deployed to live systems. To mitigate these risks, organizations should implement a staged deployment approach, applying patches to a small subset of systems first, before rolling them out across the entire network. This approach allows IT teams to monitor the patch's effectiveness and address any issues that arise before full deployment.

Despite the best efforts to avoid patch failures, they are sometimes unavoidable. Therefore, organizations must have robust contingency plans in place to address these failures when they occur. This includes having a clear rollback strategy to restore systems to their previous stable state in the event of a patch failure. Rollback procedures should be tested regularly to ensure that systems can be reverted to a secure configuration quickly and efficiently. Additionally, organizations should maintain comprehensive backup systems to ensure that critical data and system configurations are not lost during the rollback process. By having these contingency plans in place, organizations can minimize the operational impact of patch failures and reduce the risks associated with security breaches.

The risks of patch failures and breakages are significant and must be carefully evaluated as part of any organization's patch management strategy. The potential for downtime, security breaches, performance issues, and long-term vulnerabilities makes it essential for IT teams to ensure that patches are deployed correctly and consistently. By implementing robust testing, monitoring, and rollback procedures, organizations can mitigate the risks of patch failures and ensure that their systems remain secure and reliable. A proactive approach to patch management, combined with effective risk management strategies, helps to ensure that patch failures do not undermine the organization's security or operational efficiency.

Keeping Track of Software End-of-Life (EOL) and Patches

In today's fast-moving technological landscape, keeping software systems up-to-date with the latest patches is critical for maintaining security, compliance, and operational efficiency. However, one of the often overlooked yet critical aspects of patch management is keeping track of software that has reached its end-of-life (EOL). Software vendors typically provide support for their products for a specified period, after which they discontinue updates, including security patches, for the product. When software reaches its EOL, it becomes increasingly difficult to ensure that it remains secure, and failing to track and manage EOL software can expose organizations to significant risks. Understanding the implications of EOL software and actively managing its lifecycle, including patching, is crucial for organizations looking to safeguard their systems and sensitive data.

Software products are typically supported by vendors for a defined period after their initial release. This period includes regular updates and patches, including security patches that address vulnerabilities discovered in the software. However, once the software reaches its EOL, the vendor no longer provides updates, leaving the software vulnerable to newly discovered security threats. Without the ongoing support from the vendor, organizations are at a higher risk of cyberattacks and security breaches. Attackers often target software that has reached its EOL because vulnerabilities in these products are widely known and can be easily exploited. For organizations, failing to keep track of the EOL status of their software can have severe consequences, including data breaches, service disruptions, and non-compliance with regulatory standards.

Managing software at EOL involves several steps, with the most critical being the identification of when a product will reach its end of support. Many organizations have a wide range of software in use, from operating systems and office applications to specialized software solutions for different business needs. Keeping track of the support lifecycle for each product in use can be a daunting task, especially in large or complex IT environments. Without an organized approach, IT teams may struggle to track the EOL status of individual software products, which can lead to unexpected security risks when the vendor discontinues updates. This is why maintaining an accurate inventory of all software products, their versions, and their respective support lifecycles is essential.

Once software has reached EOL, organizations are faced with a critical decision: whether to continue using the software with the knowledge that it will no longer receive security patches or to upgrade or replace the software with a newer, supported version. Continuing to use EOL software exposes organizations to significant risks, as unpatched vulnerabilities become prime targets for cybercriminals. Furthermore, many regulatory frameworks require organizations to keep their systems up-to-date with the latest security patches, and failure to do so could result in non-compliance, leading to potential fines or legal consequences. While upgrading or replacing EOL software may incur costs and resource allocations, it is often the best way to ensure continued security and compliance.

Tracking software EOL is not limited to major software applications or operating systems. It also extends to smaller, less visible applications that might be embedded in other software or systems. For instance, certain plugins, utilities, or third-party libraries may reach EOL before the main application they support. Organizations need to have processes in place to track these smaller components as well. Many modern software applications are built on top of other platforms or frameworks, meaning that the EOL of one component could impact the functionality or security of the entire system. Ignoring these secondary components can create hidden vulnerabilities that remain unpatched, often unnoticed, until a security breach occurs.

When EOL software is identified, organizations must take steps to mitigate the risks associated with continuing to use it. One approach is to upgrade the software to the latest version that is still supported by the vendor. Many software vendors release new versions or updates regularly, which come with important security fixes and enhanced features. Upgrading to a supported version can help to ensure that the software remains secure and compliant with industry standards. However, upgrading is not always a straightforward process. Some software may not be easily upgradable, especially if it is deeply integrated into an organization's IT infrastructure. In these cases, IT teams need to evaluate whether it is better to replace the software entirely with a new solution that is actively supported.

Another strategy for managing EOL software is to implement additional security measures to help protect systems that continue to run unsupported software. While it is not ideal to continue using EOL software, in certain cases, it may be necessary due to budgetary constraints or other limitations. In such instances, organizations can increase their security posture by using firewalls, intrusion detection systems, and other protective measures to shield unsupported software from external threats. Network segmentation can also help isolate EOL software from more critical systems, reducing the impact of any security breach. These additional measures are not a substitute for patching and updating, but they can help to mitigate the risks associated with using EOL software for a limited period.

In addition to security concerns, keeping track of EOL software is important for ensuring business continuity and minimizing downtime. When a software product reaches EOL, vendors typically stop providing technical support, meaning that any issues or bugs discovered after the EOL date will not be addressed. This can lead to significant operational disruptions if critical software components fail or become incompatible with other systems. For example, if an organization continues to use an outdated version of an operating system or an essential business application, it may encounter difficulties when integrating with new hardware, software, or network infrastructure. By tracking EOL dates and proactively upgrading or replacing software, organizations can avoid these issues and maintain seamless business operations.

The task of managing EOL software and ensuring patching of unsupported systems is not a one-time effort but an ongoing process. IT teams must be diligent in maintaining software inventories, tracking vendor support lifecycles, and planning for future upgrades. Many organizations use software asset management (SAM) tools to automate this process, providing visibility into the software in use, its support status, and upcoming EOL dates. These tools can also help to track patching status and alert IT teams when patches are needed for both supported and unsupported software. Additionally, integrating EOL management into an organization's overall risk management and cybersecurity strategy can help ensure that patching and updates are prioritized appropriately.

An organization's approach to software EOL should be part of a broader lifecycle management strategy that aligns with its overall security and compliance goals. As software becomes outdated and unsupported, it creates a window of opportunity for attackers to exploit vulnerabilities. By keeping track of software EOL and actively managing patches, organizations can minimize these risks, maintain compliance with regulations, and ensure the long-term security and stability of their IT infrastructure. Managing the end-of-life process for software, while challenging, is an essential part of a proactive security strategy and helps organizations stay ahead of emerging threats and evolving security requirements.

Legal and Compliance Considerations in Patch Management

In the world of cybersecurity, patch management is an essential aspect of securing systems and protecting sensitive data. While patching software and operating systems may seem like a straightforward IT task, there are significant legal and compliance considerations that organizations must address when implementing their patch management strategies. Failure to adhere to legal requirements or industry standards regarding patching can result in financial penalties, legal liabilities, and damage to an organization's reputation. Therefore, understanding the intersection between patch management, legal obligations, and compliance frameworks is crucial for organizations looking to protect their data and maintain the trust of clients, partners, and regulators.

A fundamental legal consideration in patch management is ensuring that organizations comply with industry-specific regulations that mandate timely application of security patches. In highly regulated industries such as healthcare, finance, and energy, organizations are required to maintain secure systems and protect sensitive data. These regulations often specify that security patches must be applied within a certain timeframe to mitigate vulnerabilities that could lead to data breaches or unauthorized access. For instance, in healthcare, the Health Insurance Portability and Accountability Act (HIPAA) mandates that healthcare providers, insurers, and their business associates secure patient data and apply timely security updates to prevent unauthorized access. Similarly, financial institutions are required to adhere to the Payment Card Industry Data Security Standard (PCI DSS), which specifies that patches must be applied promptly to safeguard payment card information. Failing to meet these regulatory requirements by neglecting or delaying patches can result in significant legal consequences, including fines, lawsuits, and the loss of certifications or licenses.

In addition to industry-specific regulations, there are general legal principles that govern the protection of personal data. For example, the European Union's General Data Protection Regulation (GDPR) imposes strict requirements on organizations that handle the personal data of EU citizens. The GDPR emphasizes the need for organizations to take appropriate technical and organizational measures to ensure data security, which includes applying patches and updates to address vulnerabilities. Failure to apply necessary patches that protect personal data could be considered a violation of the GDPR, leading to substantial fines, legal actions, and a loss of public trust. Organizations that operate across multiple jurisdictions must also be aware of varying data protection laws and patching requirements in different countries. A patch management strategy must be flexible enough to account for the compliance needs of various regions in which an organization operates.

Compliance considerations go beyond just ensuring timely patch deployment. Organizations must also ensure that their patch management processes are well-documented and auditable. Regulatory bodies and auditors often require organizations to provide evidence of their patch management practices to demonstrate compliance with security standards. For example, PCI DSS requires organizations to maintain detailed records of patch management activities, including the identification of vulnerabilities, the patches applied, and the dates of deployment. Similarly, HIPAA requires healthcare organizations to document their efforts to secure patient data, including the implementation of security patches. These records must be readily accessible for audits and inspections, which means that organizations must have robust systems in place for tracking and documenting their patching activities. Proper documentation not only helps organizations meet compliance requirements but also ensures that they can demonstrate due diligence in protecting sensitive data during legal proceedings.

Another critical legal aspect of patch management is the responsibility for third-party software and services. Many organizations rely on third-party vendors to provide software or cloud-based services that are integral to their operations. In some cases, the responsibility for patching these third-party systems lies with the vendor, while in other cases, it is shared between the organization and the vendor. Clear contractual agreements should outline the patching responsibilities of each party to ensure that vulnerabilities are addressed in a timely manner. If a third-party service provider fails to apply patches or security updates, the organization may be held liable for any security breaches that result from the unpatched vulnerabilities. Therefore, organizations must establish clear expectations with their vendors regarding patch management and ensure that their contracts contain provisions that require vendors to maintain secure systems and apply patches promptly. This is especially important in industries where data protection regulations impose strict security requirements on both the organization and its third-party partners.

Legal considerations also extend to the risk of intellectual property theft or data breaches resulting from unpatched vulnerabilities. In many cases, unpatched systems are prime targets for cybercriminals seeking to steal sensitive information or intellectual property. Organizations that fail to manage patching properly may be held liable for damages resulting from breaches that exploit known vulnerabilities. For instance, if a patch is delayed and an attacker gains access to proprietary business information, the organization may face legal claims for negligence. Additionally, if the breach results in the exposure of personally identifiable information (PII), the organization may be subject to lawsuits from affected individuals, regulatory fines, and legal actions from consumer protection agencies. Therefore, organizations must treat patch management as part of their broader risk management strategy to reduce the likelihood of breaches and the associated legal and financial consequences.

In the event of a data breach or cyberattack resulting from a patch failure, organizations may also face reputational damage. The public perception of an organization's ability to protect data and systems is a crucial factor in maintaining customer trust and business relationships. A failure to promptly apply patches and address vulnerabilities can lead to negative media coverage, customer loss, and long-term damage to the organization's brand. Many customers and partners expect organizations to follow best practices in cybersecurity, and failure to implement an effective patch management process can signal a lack of commitment to data protection and security. In industries where consumer confidence is paramount, such as retail or financial services, reputational damage can have far-reaching consequences for an organization's long-term viability.

In some jurisdictions, organizations may be legally required to notify affected individuals in the event of a data breach. This includes providing information about the nature of the breach, the data involved, and the steps being taken to address the issue. For example, under the GDPR, organizations must notify affected individuals within 72 hours of discovering a breach. Failure to apply timely patches and resulting data breaches could lead to increased scrutiny from regulators and legal entities, along with penalties for failing to protect personal data. The legal obligation to notify stakeholders about breaches underscores the importance of having a proactive patch management strategy in place to minimize the risk of such incidents occurring in the first place.

Finally, organizations must also consider the legal implications of patch management in the context of software liability. In certain cases, patches or updates may inadvertently cause system failures or disrupt operations. If this occurs, organizations may seek legal remedies from the software vendor. However, in some cases, the vendor's terms of service may limit their liability for damages caused by patches. Understanding these terms and having a clear strategy for mitigating potential risks associated with patch deployment can help organizations avoid legal disputes and ensure they are adequately protected.

Legal and compliance considerations in patch management are vital components of an effective cybersecurity strategy. Organizations must be vigilant in ensuring that patches are applied in a timely manner to meet industry regulations, reduce security risks, and maintain compliance. Proper documentation, vendor management, and risk mitigation strategies are necessary to avoid legal liabilities, protect sensitive data, and safeguard the organization's reputation. By aligning patch management with legal and compliance requirements, organizations can create a secure, resilient infrastructure that meets regulatory standards and protects both their business and their customers.

The Role of Patch Management in Preventing Ransomware Attacks

Ransomware has become one of the most devastating and widespread cyber threats in recent years, causing significant financial and reputational damage to organizations across industries. This type of malware works by encrypting a victim's data and demanding a ransom payment in exchange for the decryption key. Often, ransomware attacks are initiated by exploiting known vulnerabilities in a system that has not been properly patched. In this context, patch management plays a crucial role in preventing ransomware attacks by closing these vulnerabilities and ensuring that systems are as secure as possible. Regular, efficient patch management is a foundational component of any cybersecurity strategy, especially in the fight against ransomware.

The first way in which patch management helps prevent ransomware attacks is by addressing known vulnerabilities. Most ransomware attacks rely on exploiting vulnerabilities in operating systems, applications, or software that have not been patched. These vulnerabilities, once identified by cybersecurity experts or the software vendor, are typically addressed by releasing a patch or an update that fixes the issue. However, if the patch is not applied in a timely manner, attackers can take advantage of the vulnerability to infiltrate the system. Many high-profile ransomware attacks, including incidents involving WannaCry and NotPetya, were caused by exploiting unpatched vulnerabilities in popular software such as Windows operating systems. The patches for these vulnerabilities had already been made available by the vendor, but many organizations failed to deploy them promptly, leaving their systems open to attack. Thus, one of the most effective ways to prevent ransomware is to ensure that patch management is consistently applied and that vulnerabilities are addressed as soon as patches are released.

Ransomware attacks often take advantage of known exploits, and the longer an organization delays patching, the higher the likelihood that attackers will target these unpatched systems. Exploits for vulnerabilities are often published and shared within cybercriminal networks, where attackers look for organizations with unpatched systems to target. This increases the window of opportunity for ransomware actors to launch their attacks. Patching software and systems regularly drastically reduces this window of exposure, significantly lowering the risk of ransomware infections. This emphasizes the importance of keeping track of patches, their release schedules, and ensuring that patches are deployed quickly, especially for critical systems and applications that are more likely to be targeted by ransomware.

Another important aspect of patch management is ensuring that both operating systems and third-party applications are updated regularly. While many organizations focus on patching the core operating systems, it is equally important to update other software and applications that could present security risks. Many ransomware attacks leverage vulnerabilities in third-party applications, such as outdated versions of web browsers, media players, or file-sharing software, to gain access to a system. Often, these applications are not subject to the same level of scrutiny and monitoring as operating systems, making them attractive targets for attackers. A comprehensive patch management strategy should include regular updates for all software components, reducing the potential for ransomware to find an entry point through vulnerable third-party applications.

The patching process also contributes to the overall hygiene of an organization's network, which is essential for preventing ransomware. A well-maintained patch management system reduces the potential for other types of malware or exploits to coexist with ransomware, further reducing the risk of a successful attack. Vulnerabilities are often interconnected, and one unpatched weakness can open the door for additional malware. By ensuring that all aspects of an organization's IT infrastructure are up-to-date, patch management not only helps to close individual security gaps but also strengthens the overall defense against ransomware and other cyber threats. A proactive approach to patching can help reduce the attack surface, which ransomware actors look to exploit.

Despite the proven benefits of patch management in preventing ransomware attacks, there are several challenges that organizations must overcome to ensure its effectiveness. One of the primary challenges is ensuring timely patch deployment across all devices in an organization's network. In modern IT environments, particularly in large organizations, managing patches for a diverse range of systems and devices, including desktops, laptops, servers, mobile devices, and IoT devices, can be a complex task. Inconsistent patching schedules, manual processes, or lack of automation can lead to delays in patch deployment, leaving systems vulnerable. A comprehensive patch management strategy should incorporate automated patching tools that ensure patches are deployed to all systems on time, reducing human error and accelerating response times. Automation tools can also help track which devices have been patched and identify those that remain vulnerable, providing real-time visibility into the status of an organization's patching efforts.

Another challenge in effective patch management is the balance between security and business continuity. While timely patch deployment is essential for preventing ransomware, patches can sometimes cause compatibility issues or system disruptions. In some cases, organizations may postpone applying patches to avoid potential disruptions to critical business operations. However, this approach carries risks, as it leaves systems unprotected and vulnerable to ransomware attacks. To address this challenge, organizations should implement a well-defined testing and staging process for patches. Before applying patches to live systems, organizations should test them in a controlled environment to ensure that they do not cause issues with other applications or systems. Staging patches before deployment allows IT teams to catch potential problems early, minimizing the risk of downtime while maintaining the security of systems.

The role of patch management extends beyond merely deploying patches to include ensuring that patches are effective and up-to-date. Even after patches are applied, the threat landscape is constantly evolving, and new vulnerabilities are discovered regularly. It is essential for organizations to stay informed about the latest security advisories and vulnerabilities and ensure that they apply updates that address newly discovered risks. Security patches are often released by vendors in response to zero-day vulnerabilities, which are previously unknown security flaws that can be exploited before they are patched. Timely application of these security updates is crucial in preventing ransomware actors from exploiting zero-day vulnerabilities, which can otherwise be used to bypass defenses and initiate attacks. Organizations must maintain a continuous awareness of patch availability and the changing cybersecurity landscape, as ransomware attackers constantly adapt their techniques to target emerging weaknesses.

Moreover, patch management for ransomware prevention requires cross-departmental coordination. Effective patching involves collaboration between the IT department, network security teams, and executive management. IT teams must prioritize critical systems and ensure that patches are deployed to these systems first, while security teams must constantly monitor for new vulnerabilities and advise on patching priorities. Management must provide the necessary resources and support to ensure that the patching process is not delayed due to competing priorities. This coordinated approach ensures that the organization's patch management strategy is comprehensive and efficient, helping to maintain system security and resilience against ransomware threats.

The importance of patch management in preventing ransomware cannot be overstated. Ransomware continues to be a top threat to organizations of all sizes, and patches are one of the most effective defenses against this pervasive malware. By addressing known vulnerabilities, reducing the attack surface, and staying up-to-date with patches, organizations can protect their systems from ransomware attacks and other cyber threats. However, effective patch management requires overcoming several challenges, including the complexity of managing diverse systems, ensuring timely deployment, and maintaining business continuity. By implementing automated patching tools, establishing robust testing procedures, and maintaining strong coordination across departments, organizations can minimize their exposure to ransomware and other security risks, creating a more secure IT environment for their operations and data.

Overcoming Resistance to Patch Updates within Organizations

In the ever-evolving landscape of cybersecurity, patch management is one of the most critical aspects of maintaining a secure IT infrastructure. Patches address vulnerabilities, improve system performance, and ensure that software remains up-to-date with the latest features. However, despite the obvious security benefits, organizations often face significant resistance when it comes to applying patch updates. This resistance can come from various sources, including employees, IT teams, or even organizational culture, and it can lead to delayed patching, leaving systems vulnerable to attacks. Overcoming this resistance is essential to ensuring that organizations remain protected from emerging threats and comply with necessary security regulations.

Resistance to patch updates often stems from a lack of understanding of the importance of patches and the risks associated with not applying them. Many employees and even IT staff may not fully grasp the potential consequences of failing to patch systems in a timely manner. Patches are frequently viewed as minor updates that may not seem urgent or necessary, especially if the system appears to be functioning well. This mindset can lead to complacency, with employees and IT staff delaying or ignoring patches. However, unpatched systems create a significant security risk, as vulnerabilities can be exploited by cybercriminals to gain unauthorized access to networks, steal sensitive data, or deploy malware. Raising awareness about the severity of the risks associated with unpatched systems is a crucial first step in overcoming resistance to patch updates within an organization.

Another major factor contributing to resistance is the perception that patching disrupts business operations. Many employees fear that applying patches will cause downtime or interfere with the functionality of critical systems. This is particularly true in organizations where patches may require system reboots or temporary disruptions to workflow. Business leaders may also be concerned about the operational impact of patching, especially in industries where downtime can result in significant financial losses or harm customer trust. While these concerns are valid, it is essential to communicate that the cost of applying patches is far less than the potential cost of dealing with a security breach or system failure caused by unpatched vulnerabilities. Organizations must implement patching strategies that minimize downtime, such as scheduling updates during off-peak hours or using staged rollouts, so that the process has as little impact on day-to-day operations as possible.

The technical complexity of applying patches can also lead to resistance, particularly in large organizations with complex IT infrastructures. In these environments, systems are often interconnected, and a patch applied to one system may affect others. IT staff may hesitate to deploy patches because of the potential for compatibility issues, bugs, or other unforeseen consequences. Additionally, the variety of operating systems, software, and hardware in use can complicate the patching process, as different systems may require different patches or configurations. The fear of introducing errors or breaking existing functionality can create resistance to patching updates. To overcome this, organizations must establish robust testing procedures for patches. By testing patches in a controlled environment before rolling them out across the entire network, IT teams can identify and address compatibility issues before they cause disruptions. This approach provides assurance that patches will not negatively impact business operations and helps build confidence in the patching process.

Another source of resistance comes from the speed at which patches are released. In many cases, patches are issued by software vendors in response to security vulnerabilities that have been identified, often after an exploit has been discovered. While vendors typically provide regular updates to fix bugs or improve features, the pace of patch releases can sometimes overwhelm IT teams, especially in organizations with large, diverse IT environments. The constant stream of patches may lead to patch fatigue, where IT staff feel overwhelmed by the volume of updates that need to be applied. This can result in delays in deploying patches, leaving systems vulnerable to attack. To address this, organizations need to prioritize patches based on their severity and the potential impact of the vulnerabilities they address. Critical patches that address high-risk vulnerabilities should be deployed immediately, while less urgent updates can be scheduled for later deployment. By establishing a clear patching policy that prioritizes patches based on their importance, IT teams can more effectively manage the patching process and avoid feeling overwhelmed.

Organizational culture also plays a significant role in resistance to patch updates. In some organizations, security may not be a top priority, and employees may not see patching as a critical task. In these cases, it is essential for leadership to set the tone and emphasize the importance of cybersecurity. Leaders must foster a culture of security awareness, where patching is viewed as an integral part of maintaining a secure and resilient IT infrastructure. This can be achieved through regular training and communication that emphasizes the risks of unpatched systems and the benefits of keeping software up-to-date. Additionally, leadership should work to ensure that patching is seen as a shared responsibility, rather than just the responsibility of the IT department. By promoting cybersecurity awareness throughout the organization, employees will be more likely to understand the importance of patching and actively support the process.

Resistance to patch updates can also arise from a lack of resources. Smaller organizations, in particular, may struggle to allocate the necessary time, budget, and personnel to manage patching effectively. IT teams in these organizations may be stretched thin, with multiple responsibilities and limited capacity to monitor and deploy patches regularly. In such cases, organizations should explore automation as a means of streamlining the patch management process. Automated patch management tools can help ensure that patches are deployed quickly and consistently across systems without requiring significant manual intervention. These tools can also provide valuable insights into patch deployment status, helping IT teams identify unpatched systems and prioritize updates accordingly. By investing in automation, organizations can reduce the burden on IT staff and improve the efficiency and effectiveness of their patching efforts.

It is also important to note that resistance to patching may stem from concerns about software stability. In some cases, organizations may avoid applying patches because they fear that updates will negatively affect the performance or stability of their systems. This is especially true for critical systems where any downtime or performance degradation could have significant consequences. While this concern is understandable, it is important to recognize that failing to apply patches can be far riskier in the long run. Patch failures and issues can be mitigated by conducting thorough testing in controlled environments, ensuring that patches do not cause adverse effects on system performance or stability before deployment. Furthermore, by keeping systems updated with the latest patches, organizations can reduce the risk of encountering security issues that could cause system failures or performance problems.

Overcoming resistance to patch updates within organizations requires a multifaceted approach. By fostering awareness of the importance of patching, addressing concerns about downtime and compatibility, and implementing automation, organizations can create an environment where patch management is seen as a critical, shared responsibility. Effective leadership, clear communication, and the strategic use of technology will help ensure that patching is integrated into the organization's overall cybersecurity strategy, reducing vulnerabilities and protecting systems from the growing threat of cyberattacks.

Patch Management for Critical Infrastructure Systems

Critical infrastructure systems are the backbone of modern society, supporting essential services like energy, transportation, healthcare, and communication. These systems are increasingly interconnected and reliant on complex IT infrastructures, which makes them attractive targets for cyberattacks. As the threat landscape continues to evolve, ensuring the security and stability of critical infrastructure is paramount. Patch management plays a vital role in safeguarding these systems by addressing vulnerabilities in operating systems, software, and hardware that could be exploited by malicious actors. However, patch management for critical infrastructure systems presents unique challenges due to the complexity, scale, and operational requirements of these systems.

Critical infrastructure systems are often designed for long-term stability and reliability, and they are typically composed of a mix of legacy systems and modern technologies. Many of these systems were not originally designed with cybersecurity in mind, and over time, they may become more vulnerable to exploits as software vulnerabilities are discovered. While patching is a common practice in traditional IT environments, patch management for critical infrastructure requires a more cautious and strategic approach. Patches must be deployed in a way that minimizes disruption to essential services and does not compromise system integrity. Given the importance of these systems, any downtime or failure resulting from poorly managed patches can have far-reaching consequences, including financial losses, safety risks, and disruption to society at large.

One of the primary challenges of patch management for critical infrastructure systems is the need to balance security with operational continuity. Many critical infrastructure systems operate 24/7 and are involved in processes that cannot be interrupted, such as power generation, water treatment, or traffic control. Patching a system may require taking it offline temporarily, which could impact its ability to function properly. For instance, a patch for an energy grid system might necessitate shutting down certain components of the grid to install the update, which could disrupt power delivery. Therefore, patch management must be meticulously planned to ensure that patches are deployed during off-peak hours or in phases, with minimal impact on operations. In some cases, a patch may need to be tested in a staging environment before being applied to production systems to ensure that it does not cause unforeseen disruptions.

Another factor complicating patch management for critical infrastructure systems is the prevalence of legacy technology. Many critical infrastructure systems are built on older hardware and software platforms that are no longer actively supported by vendors. These legacy systems may have known vulnerabilities that are not addressed by modern patches, leaving them open to attack. However, replacing or upgrading these legacy systems can be prohibitively expensive, time-consuming, and technically challenging. As a result, patching becomes even more critical for mitigating risks, but it also becomes more complex. In such cases, patch management requires a deep understanding of the systems in question and the potential risks associated with applying patches to outdated technology. Security patches for legacy systems must be thoroughly tested to ensure compatibility and stability, and there may be a need for custom patches or workarounds to address vulnerabilities in older technologies.

Another unique challenge of patch management in critical infrastructure systems is the interdependency of various components. Critical infrastructure often involves a complex web of interconnected systems, and changes to one part of the network can have unintended consequences on others. For example, a patch for a control system in a water treatment facility could have a cascading effect on other systems that rely on the data or functionality of that system. This interdependency means that patch management must be coordinated across different departments and stakeholders to ensure that all relevant systems are updated and compatible. In some cases, patching a vulnerable system could inadvertently expose another part of the infrastructure to risk, creating a new vulnerability. Therefore, a holistic approach to patch management is necessary, considering not just the system being patched but also its relationship to other critical components within the infrastructure.

Compliance and regulatory requirements are another important consideration in patch management for critical infrastructure systems. Many sectors of critical infrastructure, such as energy, transportation, and healthcare, are subject to strict regulatory oversight that mandates specific security measures, including patching. For example, the North American Electric Reliability Corporation (NERC) requires energy companies to implement cybersecurity measures, including timely patching of vulnerabilities, to protect the electric grid. Similarly, healthcare organizations are subject to regulations like the Health Insurance Portability and Accountability Act (HIPAA), which requires the protection of electronic health records (EHRs) from unauthorized access, including through timely patching of systems. Failure to comply with these regulations can result in legal and financial consequences, as well as damage to an organization's reputation. Effective patch management is, therefore, a critical component of meeting regulatory requirements and avoiding the risks associated with non-compliance.

The risk of cyberattacks on critical infrastructure has become a growing concern in recent years. Threat actors, including nation-states, cybercriminals, and hacktivists, have increasingly targeted critical infrastructure systems for espionage, disruption, or financial gain. Vulnerabilities in critical infrastructure systems are valuable targets, as an attack on these systems can cause widespread damage. Ransomware attacks, for example, have been known to target critical infrastructure systems, locking operators out of key systems and demanding ransom payments to restore access. A successful attack on a critical infrastructure system could lead to severe consequences, including public safety risks, economic losses, and damage to national security. Timely patching of vulnerabilities is an essential defense against these types of attacks. By keeping systems up to date with the latest security patches, organizations reduce the surface area available for attackers to exploit, making it more difficult for them to infiltrate the network or cause damage.

In addition to traditional IT systems, patch management for critical infrastructure must also consider industrial control systems (ICS) and supervisory control and data acquisition (SCADA) systems, which are used to monitor and control industrial processes. These systems are often integrated with physical infrastructure, such as power plants, water facilities, and transportation networks. Patching ICS and SCADA systems can be more complicated than patching traditional IT systems, as these systems often operate in isolated networks or with proprietary software. In some cases, applying a patch may require taking the system offline for a period, which could disrupt the operation of critical infrastructure. As such, organizations must carefully consider the timing and impact of patching efforts, as well as the specific requirements of ICS and SCADA systems, to minimize the risk of operational disruption.

One key strategy for improving patch management in critical infrastructure is to implement automation. Given the scale and complexity of critical infrastructure systems, manually tracking and applying patches can be an inefficient and error-prone process. Automated patch management tools can help streamline the patching process by scanning systems for vulnerabilities, identifying missing patches, and deploying updates across the infrastructure. These tools can also provide real-time visibility into patch deployment status, making it easier for IT teams to monitor progress and address any issues that arise during the patching process. Automation also ensures that patches are applied in a consistent and timely manner, reducing the risk of human error and ensuring that critical vulnerabilities are addressed promptly.

Effective patch management for critical infrastructure systems requires a well-coordinated approach that accounts for the unique challenges and risks of these systems. It involves balancing security and operational continuity, addressing legacy technologies, managing interdependencies between systems, and complying with regulatory requirements. As the threat landscape continues to evolve, organizations must remain vigilant in their patch management efforts, adopting proactive strategies and leveraging automation to ensure that critical infrastructure remains secure and resilient against emerging cyber threats. By maintaining up-to-date systems and addressing vulnerabilities before they can be exploited, organizations can help safeguard the essential services that are vital to the functioning of society.

The Interplay Between Patch Management and Network Security

Patch management and network security are two integral components of an organization's cybersecurity strategy, each contributing to the overall protection of IT systems. While they are often discussed separately, the relationship between patch management and network security is highly interconnected. Patch management ensures that software, operating systems, and applications are up to date with the latest security patches and updates, addressing known vulnerabilities. Network security, on the other hand, focuses on protecting the integrity, confidentiality, and availability of network infrastructure and data. The interplay between these two functions is vital because effective patch management directly enhances network security by reducing the number of entry points for cyberattacks. Conversely, a strong network security framework provides the foundation needed to support and safeguard the patching process.

The primary role of patch management is to mitigate risks associated with known vulnerabilities in software and systems. When vendors release patches, they address weaknesses in their products that have been identified by security researchers or attackers. These vulnerabilities can be exploited by cybercriminals to gain unauthorized access to systems, install malware, or steal sensitive data. However, applying patches is not always straightforward. Patches must be deployed across the organization's network, and the deployment process must be executed with precision to ensure that all systems are updated and remain compatible with other network components. A failure to apply patches promptly leaves systems exposed to attacks, making it easier for attackers to infiltrate the network and move laterally to other parts of the organization. Therefore, effective patch management is essential to closing security gaps and ensuring that network security is not compromised.

In the context of network security, patch management is a fundamental defense against a variety of cyber threats. Vulnerabilities in unpatched software can serve as an open door for attackers to exploit. For example, many high-profile cyberattacks, such as the WannaCry ransomware attack, were made possible by vulnerabilities that had been identified and patched by the software vendor. However, organizations that delayed or neglected to apply these patches left themselves vulnerable to attacks that could have been prevented. The delay in patching creates a window of opportunity for malicious actors to exploit known vulnerabilities, and in many cases, attacks are launched automatically by bots that scan networks for systems with unpatched vulnerabilities. By ensuring that patches are applied in a timely manner, organizations significantly reduce the attack surface available for cybercriminals to exploit.

Network security protocols, including firewalls, intrusion detection systems (IDS), and intrusion prevention systems (IPS), play an important role in protecting the network perimeter and monitoring traffic for suspicious activity. However, these measures alone are not sufficient to protect an organization from the threat of cyberattacks, especially when vulnerabilities exist within the systems themselves. Patch management acts as a complementary layer of defense to network security, closing the vulnerabilities that security devices cannot guard against. For example, a firewall may block an unauthorized connection, but if a system is running outdated software with known vulnerabilities, the attacker may be able to exploit those weaknesses to bypass the firewall. Thus, patch management is essential to fortifying the security measures already in place.

Additionally, patch management and network security work together to ensure compliance with industry regulations and standards. Many regulatory frameworks, such as the Health Insurance Portability and Accountability Act (HIPAA) or the Payment Card Industry Data Security Standard (PCI DSS), require organizations to maintain up-to-date security measures, including the application of patches. Network security is often a key component of these regulations, as it involves protecting sensitive data and maintaining the integrity of the network. By adhering to patch management policies, organizations not only improve their network security but also meet the compliance requirements set forth by regulatory bodies. Failure to apply necessary patches could result in non-compliance, leading to fines, legal consequences, and reputational damage. Thus, patch management is not only a matter of security but also of legal responsibility.

The integration of patch management with network security becomes particularly critical in environments that use a variety of devices and systems. In modern organizations, networks often include a mix of legacy systems, cloud-based services, and mobile devices, each with its own set of vulnerabilities. Ensuring that all of these components are patched in a consistent manner requires effective coordination between the patch management process and network security protocols. For instance, a vulnerability in a legacy system that is not supported by the vendor may require a different approach to patching, such as the implementation of custom security fixes or workarounds. At the same time, these legacy systems need to be protected by network security measures such as segmentation, to prevent them from becoming an entry point for attackers. Therefore, a holistic approach to patch management and network security is required to address the complexities of modern, interconnected IT environments.

The relationship between patch management and network security is also evident in the realm of incident response. When a security breach occurs, one of the first steps in the incident response process is to determine whether an unpatched vulnerability contributed to the attack. For example, if attackers gained access to the network through an unpatched system, patch management records can help investigators identify which systems were vulnerable and when patches were released. By maintaining accurate records of patch deployment and ensuring that all systems are updated regularly, organizations can respond more effectively to incidents, contain damage, and mitigate future risks. In this way, patch management acts as both a preventive measure and a critical tool in the aftermath of a security breach.

Moreover, the collaboration between patch management and network security is essential in defending against zero-day attacks, which target vulnerabilities that have not yet been identified or patched by vendors. While it is difficult to defend against zero-day exploits due to the lack of a known patch, network security systems, such as IDS and IPS, can help detect unusual behavior or traffic patterns that may indicate a zero-day attack is in progress. However, the ability to quickly patch a vulnerability once it is discovered can significantly reduce the effectiveness of zero-day exploits. In cases where a patch is released for a known vulnerability, network security measures alone may not be sufficient to prevent an attack. Applying the patch quickly can prevent the exploit from being used to compromise the network.

Another important factor in the interplay between patch management and network security is the need for constant monitoring and updating of security policies. As new vulnerabilities are discovered and patches are released, organizations must ensure that their network security protocols are updated to address these emerging threats. Regular patching helps to ensure that systems remain secure against both known and new threats, but the security measures in place, including firewalls, access controls, and encryption, must also be updated to reflect the latest security best practices. This ongoing process of patching and updating security measures helps organizations stay ahead of cyber threats and maintain a robust defense against attacks.

In summary, the interplay between patch management and network security is essential to safeguarding an organization's IT infrastructure. While network security measures provide a perimeter defense against cyberattacks, patch management addresses the vulnerabilities within systems that could be exploited by attackers. Together, these two components form a comprehensive security strategy that reduces the attack surface, mitigates risks, and ensures compliance with industry regulations. By integrating patch management into the broader network security framework, organizations can maintain secure, resilient, and compliant systems that are better equipped to withstand the evolving threat landscape.

Ensuring Consistency Across Multiple Operating Systems

In today's diverse IT environments, organizations often use a variety of operating systems (OS) across their infrastructure. These can include Windows, macOS, Linux, and even specialized systems for certain applications or hardware. Managing and ensuring consistency across these multiple operating systems is a significant challenge for IT departments. Each OS has its own architecture, patching mechanisms, and update schedules, which can make it difficult to apply security patches and updates uniformly. Ensuring that all systems, regardless of their operating system, are up-to-date and secure requires a strategic approach to patch management, system configuration, and overall IT governance. The goal is to maintain a consistent security posture while avoiding the risks associated with unpatched or outdated systems.

One of the first challenges in maintaining consistency across multiple operating systems is the differences in how patches and updates are deployed. Each operating system has its own update process. For example, Windows uses Windows Update or Windows Server Update Services (WSUS), macOS uses the App Store or enterprise deployment tools, and Linux often relies on package managers like apt or yum to deploy patches. These different methods of patching can complicate the task of ensuring that every device is properly updated in a timely manner. A patch that has been deployed to Windows devices may not automatically be applicable to macOS or Linux devices, requiring separate management processes for each OS. Additionally, different operating systems may have different patch cycles, which can create gaps in security if one system is updated before another. To overcome this challenge, organizations must establish centralized patch management tools and processes that support multiple operating systems, allowing for a unified approach to patch deployment across the entire network.

Another key aspect of ensuring consistency across operating systems is the need for comprehensive visibility and monitoring. In a multi-OS environment, it is essential to have real-time insight into the status of each system, including which patches have been applied, which are pending, and any potential issues with patch deployment. Without this visibility, IT teams risk overlooking critical updates or patches that could leave systems vulnerable. Monitoring tools that integrate with multiple operating systems can help automate the tracking of patches and updates, providing a centralized dashboard where IT teams can view the status of all devices in real-time. These tools also help identify systems that are missing critical patches, allowing IT staff to prioritize updates and ensure that all systems are in alignment with the organization's security requirements.

Consistency in patching goes beyond just applying updates—it also involves ensuring that configurations are standardized across different operating systems. Even if patches are deployed correctly, inconsistencies in system configurations can introduce vulnerabilities. For example, one system may have a firewall configuration that is more permissive than others, or an OS may have certain services running that others do not, potentially creating openings for attackers. Maintaining consistent configurations across multiple operating systems requires the use of configuration management tools that allow IT teams to define and enforce security baselines. These tools ensure that each system, regardless of its OS, adheres to the same security standards, reducing the risk of misconfigurations that could compromise the network.

In addition to configuration consistency, organizations must also address the challenge of managing different software applications across multiple operating systems. Many organizations use a mix of software that is designed for specific operating systems, and updates for these applications may also be released on different schedules. Keeping track of application updates for each OS can be a time-consuming task, especially when software patches are not automatically deployed or when applications require manual intervention for updates. To streamline this process, organizations can implement centralized software management tools that allow for the automation of software updates across different operating systems. These tools can scan for outdated applications and automatically deploy updates or notify administrators when manual intervention is needed. By ensuring that applications are consistently updated, organizations reduce the risk of vulnerabilities that may be present in outdated software.

Another critical factor in maintaining consistency is training and awareness for IT staff and end users. In environments where multiple operating systems are used, IT teams need to be proficient in managing all the systems in question. This includes understanding the nuances of patch management for each OS and being able to troubleshoot issues that may arise when updates are applied. Providing regular training to IT staff helps ensure that they are equipped to handle the complexities of multi-OS environments and can apply patches and updates effectively. End users also play a role in maintaining consistency, especially when it comes to device management. Ensuring that users understand the importance of keeping their devices up-to-date and following corporate patching policies can help prevent delays in patch deployment. Educating users about the risks of using outdated systems and the importance of system updates can encourage them to comply with organizational security policies.

The complexity of maintaining consistency across multiple operating systems is further heightened by the need for compatibility between systems. In many organizations, different operating systems are used to support various business functions. For example, Windows may be used for general office work, macOS for design or creative tasks, and Linux for server management or specialized applications. Ensuring that these systems can work together seamlessly requires careful consideration of software compatibility, network integration, and patch deployment. For instance, a patch that is applied to a Windows server might require corresponding updates to Linux-based systems that interact with it, or a macOS application might need specific configurations to run correctly on a Windows machine. Organizations must ensure that all systems are tested for compatibility after patches are applied, ensuring that no issues arise from differing OS versions or configurations.

Automating the patch management process is one of the most effective ways to ensure consistency across multiple operating systems. By leveraging automation tools, organizations can streamline the patch deployment process, reduce human error, and ensure that updates are applied consistently across all systems. Automation can be used to schedule patches during off-peak hours, ensuring minimal disruption to business operations. Additionally, automated patch management tools can be configured to handle multiple operating systems, providing a centralized solution for managing patches across diverse environments. These tools also allow for automated rollback in case of patch failure, ensuring that systems can be restored to a stable state if an update causes issues.

Lastly, regular auditing and reporting are essential to maintaining consistency in patch management. By conducting regular audits, organizations can verify that patches have been deployed properly, configurations are standardized, and systems remain secure across all operating systems. These audits also provide an opportunity to identify gaps in the patch management process and make improvements where necessary. Reports generated from patch management systems can provide valuable insights into the status of updates, helping IT teams track progress, monitor compliance, and identify areas for improvement.

Ensuring consistency across multiple operating systems is a multifaceted challenge that requires careful planning, coordination, and execution. From patch deployment to configuration management, organizations must adopt a comprehensive approach that accounts for the complexities of different OS environments. By leveraging automated tools, maintaining strong visibility, and providing ongoing training, organizations can create a cohesive patch management strategy that enhances security and reduces vulnerabilities across all systems.

Managing Patches in Highly Sensitive Data Environments

In organizations that handle highly sensitive data, such as financial institutions, healthcare providers, government agencies, and research facilities, the management of patches is of paramount importance. These environments are prime targets for cyberattacks, and any vulnerability in their systems can lead to significant risks, including data breaches, intellectual property theft, and violations of legal and regulatory obligations. The need for effective patch management is even more critical in these settings, where the data at stake can have profound implications for privacy, security, and trust. Managing patches in highly sensitive data environments requires a strategic approach, as the challenges faced are more complex due to the high value of the data, the increased scrutiny of regulatory compliance, and the potential impact of downtime or disruptions.

One of the primary considerations in managing patches for sensitive data environments is ensuring that all systems are kept up-to-date with the latest security patches, while minimizing the risks associated with patch deployment. The primary purpose of patches is to fix security vulnerabilities that could be exploited by malicious actors. In highly

160

sensitive data environments, vulnerabilities in software or systems are particularly critical because an exploit could lead to unauthorized access to confidential data, financial information, or personal health records. Applying patches quickly and efficiently is essential to reduce the window of opportunity for attackers. However, patching must be done carefully to avoid introducing new risks. For example, some patches may cause system instability, compatibility issues, or operational disruptions, especially in complex environments. A patch that causes downtime in a mission-critical system could compromise the integrity of business operations and cause data loss. Therefore, a well-planned and tested patch management strategy is essential to ensure that patches are deployed without negatively impacting the functioning of critical systems.

In highly sensitive data environments, the security of data during patch deployment is a top priority. Patching activities must be performed in a way that does not expose sensitive data to unauthorized access or compromise its confidentiality and integrity. During patch deployment, it is essential to maintain strict access controls, encrypt data where necessary, and monitor systems for any signs of unusual activity. Patching processes should be done in secure environments with proper authentication and authorization mechanisms to ensure that only authorized personnel are applying patches and making changes to sensitive systems. Additionally, patch management tools should be configured to track every change made to the system, providing an audit trail that can be reviewed in the event of a security incident or compliance audit.

For organizations handling sensitive data, regulatory compliance is another critical factor in patch management. Various regulations, such as the Health Insurance Portability and Accountability Act (HIPAA) for healthcare organizations, the General Data Protection Regulation (GDPR) for organizations in the European Union, and the Payment Card Industry Data Security Standard (PCI DSS) for financial institutions, impose strict requirements regarding data security and patch management. These regulations often require that patches be applied in a timely manner to mitigate vulnerabilities that could lead to breaches of sensitive information. Compliance with these standards requires organizations to implement patch management procedures that ensure patches are deployed promptly, and detailed records are maintained to demonstrate that patching efforts are in line with regulatory requirements. In highly sensitive data environments, failure to apply patches in a timely manner can result in substantial fines, reputational damage, and the loss of customer trust. Therefore, organizations must not only prioritize patching but also establish clear policies and procedures that document their compliance with relevant laws and regulations.

One of the unique challenges in managing patches in these environments is the complexity of the IT infrastructure. Many organizations that handle sensitive data operate large, heterogeneous IT environments that include a mix of operating systems, software applications, network devices, and third-party services. Managing patches across such a diverse set of systems requires careful coordination to ensure that all systems are patched consistently. This can be especially challenging when dealing with legacy systems that are no longer supported by vendors or when different software applications rely on distinct patching schedules. Organizations need to ensure that patch management tools are capable of handling these complexities by providing centralized visibility into the status of all systems, regardless of the underlying platform. Automated patch management systems are particularly valuable in these environments, as they can help streamline the patching process by automatically detecting missing patches, scheduling updates, and ensuring that patches are deployed consistently across all systems.

The process of testing patches before deployment is also critical in highly sensitive data environments. Due to the high stakes involved, it is essential to thoroughly test patches in a staging environment before they are deployed to live systems. Patches can sometimes have unintended side effects, causing system crashes, data corruption, or compatibility issues with other applications. Testing patches in a controlled environment allows organizations to identify potential problems and resolve them before patches are deployed to production systems. Additionally, staging patches helps to ensure that the updated systems will function as expected and that critical data remains intact. The testing process should simulate real-world scenarios, taking into account the specific configurations of the systems involved and the business processes that rely on them. This testing phase is crucial for ensuring that patch deployment does not disrupt operations or compromise the security and integrity of sensitive data.

Another key consideration in managing patches in sensitive environments is the need for effective communication and coordination across departments. Patch management is often the responsibility of IT teams, but in highly regulated environments, it also involves collaboration with other departments such as legal, compliance, and risk management. These departments must be kept informed about patching schedules, compliance requirements, and any potential risks associated with deploying patches. Regular communication between teams helps ensure that patch management activities align with broader organizational goals, such as maintaining business continuity and protecting sensitive data. Additionally, when applying patches to systems that handle sensitive data, it is important to coordinate with stakeholders to ensure that patches are deployed at the most appropriate times, minimizing the impact on daily operations.

The rapid pace of emerging threats and vulnerabilities in today's cybersecurity landscape also requires organizations to adopt an agile approach to patch management. Cybercriminals are constantly looking for ways to exploit newly discovered vulnerabilities, and zero-day attacks, in which attackers exploit unknown vulnerabilities before a patch is available, are a growing concern. In highly sensitive data environments, the ability to quickly apply patches in response to new vulnerabilities is critical. Organizations must have a responsive patch management system in place that can react quickly to security advisories and deploy patches as soon as they are released. This requires a combination of real-time monitoring, automated patch deployment, and effective communication with vendors to stay ahead of emerging threats.

Managing patches in highly sensitive data environments is a multifaceted challenge that requires careful planning, coordination, and execution. Organizations must balance the need for security with the need to maintain operational continuity and ensure compliance with regulatory requirements. A comprehensive patch management strategy, which includes thorough testing, automation, and effective collaboration, is essential for maintaining the security and integrity of sensitive systems and data. By prioritizing patch management, organizations can mitigate the risks posed by vulnerabilities, ensure that they remain compliant with industry standards, and protect their valuable data assets from potential threats.

Building a Patch Management Framework for Global Organizations

In today's interconnected world, global organizations face unique challenges in managing their IT infrastructure. With offices and operations spread across multiple regions and countries, the need for effective and consistent patch management becomes critical. Patch management ensures that all systems are updated with the latest security patches, software updates, and bug fixes, but the complexity of managing patches across different time zones, regions, and compliance requirements adds a layer of difficulty. A robust patch management framework is essential for maintaining the security and integrity of global IT systems, protecting sensitive data, and ensuring compliance with diverse regulatory requirements. Building such a framework requires careful planning, coordination, and alignment with organizational objectives.

A fundamental element of building a patch management framework for a global organization is creating standardized policies and processes that can be adapted across different regions. While each office or operation may have its unique requirements, a centralized approach ensures that patches are applied consistently and efficiently. Standardizing policies helps ensure that all systems, regardless of their location, are subject to the same security measures and timelines. A standardized framework also simplifies the patch management process by establishing clear roles, responsibilities, and timelines for patch deployment. This is particularly important in large organizations where IT teams may be distributed across multiple locations and may need to collaborate on patching efforts. Standardization ensures that no system is left behind and that critical patches are applied across the entire network without delays.

However, while standardization is essential, it is equally important to account for regional differences when building a patch management framework for a global organization. Different countries have varying regulatory requirements, compliance standards, and data protection laws that may influence how patches are deployed. For instance, the European Union's General Data Protection Regulation (GDPR) imposes strict rules on the handling of personal data, and organizations operating in the EU must ensure that their patch management practices comply with these regulations. Similarly, countries like the United States have sector-specific regulations, such as the Health Insurance Portability and Accountability Act (HIPAA) for healthcare providers, that govern how systems must be secured, including timely patching of vulnerabilities. A successful patch management framework must incorporate local legal and compliance considerations to ensure that patches are deployed in a way that meets the requirements of each jurisdiction.

Effective patch management for global organizations also requires centralized visibility and reporting. With multiple offices and locations around the world, it is crucial for IT teams to have real-time visibility into the status of patches across the entire infrastructure. Centralized monitoring tools allow IT administrators to track which systems have been patched, which are pending updates, and which systems may be out of compliance. These tools can also provide detailed reports on the patching process, helping organizations to audit their patch management efforts and demonstrate compliance with industry regulations. Centralized visibility also enables IT teams to prioritize patching efforts, ensuring that the most critical systems and vulnerabilities are addressed first. In global organizations, where there may be differing levels of expertise and resources across regions, centralized reporting ensures that patch management is carried out efficiently and according to plan.

In addition to centralized visibility, automation plays a crucial role in building a patch management framework for global organizations. Manual patching processes are not only time-consuming but also prone to human error. Automating patch deployment allows organizations to ensure that patches are applied consistently and promptly across all systems, regardless of location. Automation tools can be set to deploy patches automatically, schedule updates during off-peak hours to minimize disruption, and roll back patches if any issues arise. This reduces the burden on IT teams, particularly in large organizations with a complex IT infrastructure, and helps to ensure that critical patches are applied without delay. Automation also enhances compliance by ensuring that patches are deployed on time and according to the organization's policies, reducing the risk of missed updates or vulnerabilities being left unaddressed.

Collaboration between regional IT teams and centralized patch management teams is also essential when building a global patch management framework. While centralization provides oversight and consistency, local IT teams are often more familiar with the specific systems and operational needs of their regions. It is important to foster a collaborative environment where local teams can provide input on patch deployment schedules, potential system impacts, and compliance requirements. Local teams may also have valuable insights into the unique challenges of deploying patches in their regions, such as language barriers, network constraints, or hardware compatibility issues. By working together, regional and central teams can ensure that patches are deployed efficiently, minimizing disruption and addressing any unique requirements.

Security is a critical concern in patch management, especially for global organizations. In sensitive environments, such as those dealing with personal data, financial information, or intellectual property, patch management plays a key role in protecting against cyber threats. Vulnerabilities that remain unpatched can expose systems to attacks, including malware infections, data breaches, and ransomware. For global organizations, the potential impact of a successful attack can be severe, leading to reputational damage, financial loss, and legal penalties. Patch management must, therefore, be part of a broader security strategy, with patching efforts aligned with other security measures, such as network monitoring, threat intelligence, and incident response planning. Ensuring that patches are deployed promptly and consistently helps to reduce the risk of successful cyberattacks, while regular vulnerability assessments and penetration testing can help identify additional areas that require patching.

Finally, the patch management framework for a global organization must be flexible enough to adapt to future changes. As organizations grow and evolve, so too will their IT infrastructure and security requirements. New technologies, systems, and applications may be introduced, each with its own patching needs. A flexible framework allows organizations to scale their patch management efforts and integrate new systems seamlessly into the existing process. This adaptability is crucial for addressing the increasing complexity of global IT environments, where the pace of technological change is accelerating, and new vulnerabilities are constantly emerging. Ensuring that the patch management framework is agile and responsive to these changes is key to maintaining the organization's security posture over time.

Building a patch management framework for a global organization is a multifaceted process that requires careful coordination, clear policies, and the right tools. By standardizing processes, ensuring compliance with regional regulations, leveraging automation, and fostering collaboration, organizations can create a robust and effective patch management strategy. This approach not only strengthens security but also ensures that the organization can respond quickly to emerging threats, minimize operational disruptions, and maintain compliance with global regulatory requirements. A well-designed patch management framework is an essential component of a global organization's cybersecurity strategy, safeguarding its IT infrastructure and sensitive data from the evolving threat landscape.

Understanding and Managing Software Vulnerability Databases

In the ever-evolving landscape of cybersecurity, managing software vulnerabilities is one of the most critical tasks for organizations striving to protect their digital infrastructure. Software vulnerabilities are weaknesses in a system that can be exploited by cybercriminals to gain unauthorized access, cause disruptions, or compromise sensitive data. To effectively manage these vulnerabilities, organizations rely heavily on software vulnerability databases. These databases serve as centralized repositories that catalog known vulnerabilities in various software products and provide detailed information about their risks, exploits, and mitigation strategies. Understanding and managing these databases is essential for maintaining a robust cybersecurity posture and ensuring timely responses to potential threats.

A software vulnerability database is a crucial resource for identifying, tracking, and addressing security weaknesses in software applications, operating systems, and other digital assets. These databases compile vulnerabilities that have been discovered by security researchers, software vendors, or independent entities. They typically provide details about the nature of each vulnerability, including its severity, affected software versions, potential exploits, and the availability of patches or workarounds. Some well-known vulnerability databases include the National Vulnerability Database (NVD), the Common Vulnerabilities and Exposures (CVE) system, and the Open Web Application Security Project (OWASP) Vulnerability Database. Each of these platforms serves a similar purpose: to catalog known vulnerabilities and provide detailed, up-to-date information that organizations can use to secure their systems.

The first step in managing software vulnerabilities is understanding the types of information provided by these databases. Vulnerability entries typically contain a range of key details, including a unique identifier (such as a CVE number), a description of the vulnerability, the affected software versions, and an assessment of the vulnerability's severity. The severity of a vulnerability is often indicated by a Common Vulnerability Scoring System (CVSS) score, which ranges from 0 to 10. A higher score indicates a more critical vulnerability that poses a greater risk to system security. In addition to these details, vulnerability databases may include information on potential exploits, references to security advisories, and patches or workarounds provided by the vendor to mitigate the risk. By leveraging this information, organizations can assess which vulnerabilities pose the greatest threat to their systems and prioritize patching efforts accordingly.

One of the challenges of managing vulnerabilities is the sheer volume of data available in these databases. With thousands of vulnerabilities cataloged annually, it can be difficult for IT and security teams to determine which vulnerabilities to address first. Vulnerability databases are typically searchable and allow for filtering based on factors such as severity, software version, and exploitability. By leveraging these features, organizations can focus on addressing the most critical vulnerabilities first, based on their impact on the organization's operations and security posture. However, it is important to understand that not all vulnerabilities will be applicable to every organization. For example, a vulnerability in a software version that is not used by the organization may not need immediate attention, while vulnerabilities in widely used software or systems should be prioritized for patching.

Managing software vulnerability databases also involves monitoring and responding to new vulnerabilities as they are discovered. As cyber threats continue to evolve, new vulnerabilities are discovered regularly, and it is crucial for organizations to stay informed about emerging risks. This requires a proactive approach to vulnerability management, which includes subscribing to vulnerability alerts, regularly reviewing vulnerability databases, and integrating the information into the organization's security practices. Vulnerability alerts are often provided by vendors, security researchers, and government agencies and serve as a way to notify organizations about new vulnerabilities and patches. By staying informed about the latest vulnerabilities, organizations can act quickly to deploy patches or mitigate risks before they are exploited.

The process of managing software vulnerabilities goes beyond simply identifying and addressing known issues. It also involves developing a comprehensive vulnerability management strategy that integrates vulnerability database information into the broader security framework. Vulnerability management should be closely tied to patch management, risk assessment, and incident response processes. For example, when a new vulnerability is discovered and added to a database, the vulnerability management team should assess its relevance to the organization's systems and prioritize patching based on severity and potential impact. Additionally, security teams should be prepared to respond to exploits of unpatched vulnerabilities by having an incident response plan in place. This may involve isolating affected systems, applying temporary mitigations, and coordinating with vendors or security experts to address the issue.

Another key aspect of managing vulnerability databases is ensuring compliance with industry regulations and standards. Many industries, such as healthcare, finance, and government, are subject to strict data protection regulations that require organizations to implement security measures to protect against known vulnerabilities. These regulations may include requirements for timely patching, vulnerability scanning, and risk assessments. Failure to address vulnerabilities in a timely manner can result in legal penalties, fines, or reputational damage. By using software vulnerability databases to stay informed about vulnerabilities and applying patches or mitigations in accordance with regulatory requirements, organizations can demonstrate compliance and avoid potential legal consequences.

Furthermore, vulnerability databases play a vital role in supporting continuous improvement in an organization's cybersecurity posture. By analyzing trends in vulnerabilities and attack patterns, organizations can identify areas where their security practices may be lacking and take steps to strengthen defenses. For example, if a particular type of vulnerability is repeatedly exploited, it may indicate a weakness in the organization's security architecture or a failure to apply certain types of patches. By using vulnerability database information to inform security assessments and audits, organizations can continuously improve their security measures and reduce the likelihood of future vulnerabilities being exploited.

In addition to internal vulnerability management, organizations should also collaborate with external stakeholders, including software vendors, cybersecurity experts, and other organizations, to share information about vulnerabilities and security threats. Many vulnerability databases are collaborative efforts that involve contributions from multiple sources, including security researchers, vendors, and government agencies. By actively participating in these communities and sharing insights and best practices, organizations can benefit from collective knowledge and stay ahead of emerging threats.

The management of software vulnerabilities in highly dynamic and complex IT environments is a continuous challenge. Leveraging the power of vulnerability databases is essential for identifying risks, prioritizing patching efforts, and ensuring a comprehensive approach to cybersecurity. The integration of vulnerability management with other cybersecurity practices, such as incident response, risk management, and compliance, helps organizations minimize the impact of security threats and maintain the integrity of their systems and data. A strategic approach to vulnerability database management ensures that organizations are well-equipped to respond to the ever-changing landscape of cybersecurity threats, enhancing their resilience and ability to safeguard critical assets.

The Cost of Poor Patch Management: Financial and Operational Impact

Patch management is a fundamental aspect of cybersecurity and IT operations, designed to address vulnerabilities, enhance system performance, and ensure the continued functionality of software applications. However, when patch management practices are inadequate or neglected, the consequences can be both financially and operationally devastating for an organization. From data breaches and regulatory penalties to operational downtime and damage to customer trust, the costs of poor patch management can be far-reaching. Understanding the financial and operational impact of failing to maintain effective patch management systems is critical for organizations to prioritize and invest in this crucial aspect of IT security.

One of the most immediate financial consequences of poor patch management is the increased likelihood of security breaches. Unpatched systems present a prime target for cybercriminals who are looking to exploit known vulnerabilities. These vulnerabilities are frequently cataloged and disclosed in software vulnerability databases, and when vendors release patches, they provide organizations with an opportunity to address these risks. However, organizations that fail to apply these patches in a timely manner leave their systems exposed to attacks. Cyberattacks resulting from unpatched vulnerabilities can lead to direct financial losses, including theft of sensitive data, intellectual property, or financial resources. In some cases, attackers may use compromised systems to initiate ransomware attacks, locking the organization out of critical systems until a ransom is paid. The costs of these attacks can range from the immediate ransom payment to the long-term expense of recovering from a data breach, including incident response, forensic investigations, and public relations efforts.

The financial repercussions extend well beyond the initial costs associated with a breach. Organizations that experience data breaches due to poor patch management often face significant regulatory penalties. Many industries are governed by stringent regulations concerning data protection and privacy, such as the General Data Protection Regulation (GDPR) in the European Union, the Health Insurance Portability and Accountability Act (HIPAA) in the United States, or the Payment Card Industry Data Security Standard (PCI DSS) in the financial sector. These regulations often require organizations to implement reasonable security measures, including timely patching, to protect sensitive data. When patch management is neglected, and a breach occurs, organizations may face heavy fines for non-compliance with these regulations. In some cases, fines can run into millions of dollars, depending on the severity of the breach and the regulatory framework governing the organization. The cost of fines, coupled with the costs of remediation, legal fees, and reputational damage, can significantly harm an organization's financial health.

Beyond financial penalties, poor patch management can lead to long-term reputational damage. Customer trust is paramount for any business, and once it is compromised, it can take years to rebuild. When customers' personal data, financial information, or proprietary business data is exposed due to unpatched vulnerabilities, they are less likely to trust the organization in the future. This is particularly true in industries such as banking, healthcare, and e-commerce, where customers expect the highest level of security. If news of a data breach spreads, it can erode confidence in the organization's ability to safeguard sensitive information, leading to customer churn and a loss of business. The cost of losing customers, as well as the expense involved in retaining and attracting new clients, can significantly affect the bottom line. Furthermore, a damaged reputation can affect relationships with partners, suppliers, and investors, who may choose to sever ties with an organization perceived as negligent in its security practices.

In addition to the direct financial costs associated with cyberattacks and breaches, poor patch management can result in significant operational disruptions. Systems that are not regularly patched are more likely to experience performance issues, such as system crashes, slowdowns, or instability. These issues can interfere with daily business operations, causing delays and inefficiencies. For instance, if an unpatched server crashes due to a known vulnerability, employees may be unable to access critical systems, leading to downtime and lost productivity. This operational disruption can be especially detrimental in industries where uptime is crucial, such as manufacturing, telecommunications, and financial services. The longer the downtime lasts, the greater the impact on business continuity, with the potential for lost revenue, missed deadlines, and decreased service levels.

The indirect costs of operational disruption can also be significant. For instance, when a system goes down due to an unpatched vulnerability, IT teams must divert resources to address the issue, which can lead to delays in other important tasks or projects. Additionally, employees who rely on the affected system may have to find alternative ways of performing their work, which can increase inefficiency and reduce productivity across the organization. In the worst cases, patch-related disruptions can extend to customer-facing systems, leading to delays in service delivery, customer complaints, and ultimately, a loss of business. The time and resources spent on recovering from patching issues and resolving system instability could otherwise have been used to improve business operations or develop new products and services.

Another operational impact of poor patch management is the increased complexity and cost of future remediation efforts. When patches are deferred or ignored, vulnerabilities accumulate over time, making it more difficult to address them all at once. As the number of unpatched systems increases, the complexity of patching grows, requiring more time, resources, and effort to apply updates and fixes across the entire infrastructure. This can lead to bottlenecks and delays in patch deployment, which can prolong the exposure to potential exploits. Furthermore, the cost of remediation increases as vulnerabilities age, as more sophisticated security measures may be required to mitigate their effects. Instead of dealing with a manageable number of vulnerabilities, IT teams may find themselves addressing a backlog of patching tasks that require substantial resources to fix. The longer an organization delays patching, the more expensive and time-consuming it becomes to remedy the situation, further escalating the operational burden.

In some cases, poor patch management may also increase the likelihood of cascading failures within an organization's IT infrastructure. For example, if a critical system is left unpatched and compromised, it can create a domino effect, leading to further system failures or network disruptions. The interconnected nature of modern IT systems means that a vulnerability in one area can quickly spread across the network, impacting multiple systems and services. The cost of addressing these cascading failures is much higher than simply applying patches in a timely manner, as organizations may need to perform widespread system restorations, replace damaged hardware, or even rebuild entire networks.

Finally, the long-term financial costs of poor patch management can include increased insurance premiums. Cybersecurity insurance is becoming increasingly important for organizations looking to protect themselves against the financial impact of cyberattacks. However, insurance providers often require organizations to demonstrate that they have implemented adequate security measures, including patch management practices. Organizations that fail to manage their patches properly may face higher premiums or even be denied coverage altogether. The increased risk of a breach due to poor patching practices makes organizations more vulnerable to attacks, which insurance providers factor into their pricing.

In sum, the cost of poor patch management is a multifaceted issue that affects an organization's financial health, operational efficiency, and reputation. Cyberattacks, regulatory fines, lost customers, operational disruptions, and increased remediation costs can all result from failing to apply patches in a timely and effective manner. By investing in robust patch management processes and ensuring that vulnerabilities are addressed promptly, organizations can mitigate these risks, protect their assets, and maintain a secure and reliable IT infrastructure.

Using Machine Learning to Enhance Patch Management Practices

In today's rapidly evolving cybersecurity landscape, patch management has become a cornerstone of organizational security. Patches are released to fix vulnerabilities, improve system performance, and ensure compliance with regulatory requirements. However, the sheer volume of patches and the complexity of managing them across diverse IT environments can overwhelm traditional methods of patch management. In response to this challenge, machine learning (ML) has emerged as a powerful tool to enhance patch management practices. By leveraging machine learning algorithms, organizations can improve patch deployment efficiency, predict vulnerabilities, automate patch prioritization, and reduce human error, making patch management both more effective and scalable.

Machine learning's role in patch management starts with its ability to analyze vast amounts of data to identify patterns that would otherwise be difficult for humans to detect. A key challenge in traditional patch management is knowing when and where to apply patches, particularly in complex systems with multiple software applications, operating systems, and third-party services. Manual patch management often involves IT teams scanning vulnerability databases and security advisories to identify patches, a process that is not only time-consuming but prone to oversight. Machine learning models, however, can continuously monitor system health and security, analyzing data from various sources, including threat intelligence feeds, vulnerability databases, and past incidents, to predict where vulnerabilities are most likely to occur. This predictive capability allows organizations to proactively address vulnerabilities before they are exploited, ensuring a more efficient patching process.

In addition to predicting vulnerabilities, machine learning can enhance the prioritization of patches. Not all vulnerabilities carry the same level of risk, and not all patches need to be applied immediately. Prioritizing patches based on their severity, potential impact, and the criticality of the affected systems is essential for minimizing risk without unnecessarily disrupting business operations. Machine learning algorithms can analyze historical data on cyberattacks, vulnerability exploitability, and system configurations to determine which patches should be prioritized. These algorithms can consider factors such as the likelihood of exploitation, the system's exposure to the internet, and the system's role within the organization's infrastructure. By using this data-driven approach, organizations can focus their efforts on the most critical patches and avoid wasting resources on less impactful vulnerabilities.

Moreover, machine learning can help automate patch deployment. Traditionally, patching has been a manual process, requiring significant effort from IT staff to test, deploy, and verify patches across systems. This process is not only labor-intensive but also prone to human error, with missed patches or incorrect patching potentially leaving systems vulnerable to attacks. Machine learning can streamline this process by automating the deployment of patches. Once patches are released and tested, machine learning systems can determine the best time to deploy patches based on system activity and network traffic. By scheduling patches during off-peak hours and ensuring that they are deployed systematically, organizations can minimize downtime and disruptions while maintaining security. Automation also ensures that patches are applied consistently across all systems, reducing the risk of vulnerabilities slipping through the cracks.

Machine learning also enables organizations to improve the testing of patches before deployment. A common concern with patching is that patches, while designed to address vulnerabilities, can sometimes cause issues with system functionality or compatibility. Unintended consequences, such as software crashes or performance degradation, can occur when patches are deployed to complex systems. Machine learning algorithms can simulate patch deployments in controlled environments, testing them across various configurations to predict how they will interact with different systems and software. This allows organizations to identify potential issues before patches are applied to live systems, ensuring that patch deployment does not disrupt business operations. By using machine learning to automate the testing process, organizations can speed up patch deployments without compromising system integrity.

Another advantage of machine learning in patch management is its ability to continuously learn and improve based on new data. As patches are applied and vulnerabilities are addressed, machine learning models can refine their predictions and patching strategies based on the outcomes of past deployments. This feedback loop allows machine learning algorithms to improve their accuracy in predicting vulnerabilities, prioritizing patches, and identifying potential risks. Over time, machine learning systems become more adept at understanding an organization's unique IT environment, making patch management even more efficient and tailored to the specific needs of the business. This continuous learning process also helps organizations stay ahead of emerging threats, as machine learning models can adapt to the evolving nature of cybersecurity risks.

Furthermore, machine learning can improve communication and collaboration between security teams, IT operations, and management. With machine learning, organizations can generate real-time reports and dashboards that provide clear insights into patch deployment status, system vulnerabilities, and patching progress. These dashboards can be tailored to different stakeholders, such as executives who need a high-level overview of patching efforts or IT teams that need detailed technical information. By providing actionable insights and visualizations, machine learning enables better decision-making and more efficient resource allocation. This transparency also helps security teams collaborate more effectively, as they can access up-to-date information about system health and potential risks.

However, the implementation of machine learning in patch management is not without its challenges. First, it requires a significant investment in technology and infrastructure to collect, store, and analyze the vast amounts of data needed to train machine learning models. Organizations must also ensure that their data is accurate and comprehensive, as machine learning models are only as good as the data they are trained on. Inaccurate or incomplete data can lead to flawed predictions and ineffective patching strategies. Additionally, machine learning models must be continuously updated and monitored to ensure that they remain relevant as new vulnerabilities and threats emerge. Despite these challenges, the benefits of integrating machine learning into patch management far outweigh the potential drawbacks, especially as the volume and complexity of software vulnerabilities continue to increase.

Finally, machine learning can play a role in enhancing an organization's overall cybersecurity posture by integrating with other security measures. Patch management is just one aspect of an organization's broader security strategy. By combining machine learning with other technologies, such as threat intelligence platforms, intrusion detection systems, and network monitoring tools, organizations can create a more cohesive and proactive security framework. Machine learning can help identify emerging threats, provide context for patch prioritization, and ensure that vulnerabilities are addressed in a timely manner. This integrated approach allows organizations to stay ahead of cybercriminals, minimize their exposure to risk, and protect critical assets from attacks.

In conclusion, the use of machine learning to enhance patch management practices represents a significant advancement in cybersecurity. By leveraging machine learning, organizations can improve the efficiency and effectiveness of their patching efforts, reducing the risk of security breaches and ensuring the integrity of their systems. Through predictive capabilities, automation, and continuous learning, machine learning can help organizations keep their systems secure while minimizing operational disruptions. As cyber threats become more sophisticated and complex, the integration of machine learning into patch management will be essential for maintaining a strong and resilient security posture.

Managing Patch Updates for Virtual Machines and Containers

In today's rapidly evolving IT environments, virtualization and containerization have become core components of many organizations' infrastructure strategies. Virtual machines (VMs) and containers offer a flexible and scalable way to deploy applications and manage resources across multiple environments. However, as organizations increasingly adopt these technologies, the complexity of patch management grows significantly. The dynamic nature of VMs and containers, their widespread use in cloud environments, and the need to ensure security across a variety of platforms make patching these technologies both essential and challenging. Effective patch management for VMs and containers requires a comprehensive approach that includes timely updates, rigorous testing, automation, and robust tracking systems to ensure consistency and security.

Virtual machines and containers share the fundamental challenge of requiring consistent patching to ensure the systems they run on are secure. VMs, which emulate entire physical computers with an operating system (OS), often run multiple applications and services on top of an underlying hypervisor. Containers, on the other hand, provide a lightweight alternative to VMs by virtualizing the operating system, running applications in isolated environments that share the host system's OS kernel. Both of these technologies are prone to security vulnerabilities, and if patches are not applied promptly, they can become easy targets for cybercriminals. The primary challenge in managing patch updates for these systems lies in their dynamic and distributed nature. Unlike traditional physical machines, VMs and containers can be spun up and torn down at a rapid pace, meaning that patching needs to be done in a highly automated and continuous manner to avoid gaps in security.

In the case of virtual machines, patch management involves not only patching the guest operating system but also the underlying hypervisor and the host system. The hypervisor is a key component in virtualization, responsible for managing the creation, execution, and operation of virtual machines. A vulnerability in the hypervisor could allow attackers to escape the VM and access the underlying host system or other VMs running on the same host. Thus, it is crucial to apply patches to both the guest OS and the hypervisor in parallel. This dual-layer patching requirement increases the complexity of the patch management process, especially in large-scale environments with numerous VMs spread across different regions or cloud environments. For example, in a private cloud environment, the hypervisor patches must be applied to the host machines, followed by guest OS patches on the individual virtual machines. In some cases, updates may even require coordination between cloud providers and in-house IT teams to ensure all patches are deployed effectively.

Containers, while generally easier to manage than VMs due to their lightweight nature, also present unique challenges in patch management. Containers typically use base images, which are pre-configured operating system environments on which applications run. These images, much like VMs, must be kept up-to-date to avoid security vulnerabilities. Patching containers requires not only updating the base images but also ensuring that all the containers running from those images are updated accordingly. A challenge arises in containerized environments because containers are often ephemeral in nature—they are deployed, scaled, and destroyed quickly, making it harder to track and manage their patching status. Furthermore, container images may pull their dependencies from different sources, which adds another layer of complexity in ensuring that all dependencies are also updated regularly.

One of the main advantages of both virtual machines and containers is their portability. These technologies allow organizations to move workloads seamlessly between different environments, such as from on-premises data centers to public or private clouds. However, this portability also complicates patch management, as different environments may have different patching mechanisms and schedules. For example, a VM running in an on-premises data center might be patched using a traditional Windows Update system, while the same VM, when migrated to a cloud environment, may rely on a cloud provider's patching system. Containers present similar issues; containers running in Kubernetes clusters in one cloud environment might need different patching strategies compared to those running in another cloud provider's infrastructure.

To effectively manage patch updates across virtual machines and containers, organizations must implement a centralized patch management system that provides visibility across all environments. This system should be capable of managing patches for the guest operating systems, the hypervisor, the host systems, and the container base images. Automation is key in this regard. Automated patch management tools can continuously monitor for new vulnerabilities and patches, automatically deploying them across VMs and containers as needed. These tools can ensure that patches are applied in a timely manner and that all systems are updated simultaneously, reducing the risk of vulnerabilities being exploited. Additionally, automation tools can schedule patching during off-peak hours to minimize disruption to operations, particularly in environments that require high availability.

Another important component of managing patch updates for virtual machines and containers is testing. Before deploying patches to live environments, it is essential to test them in isolated environments to ensure that they do not introduce compatibility issues, system instability, or downtime. Testing patches in a staging environment mimics the production environment and helps identify potential problems before they impact the organization. For both VMs and containers, testing should include not only the updates to the guest OS or container images but also any dependencies or configurations that might be affected by the patch. In a containerized environment, this could mean testing updates to base images, application containers, and their interactions with other containerized services.

Tracking and documenting patching efforts is another critical element of managing patch updates for virtual machines and containers. Given the large number of systems in dynamic environments, organizations must maintain comprehensive records of which patches have been applied to which systems and when. This documentation is vital for compliance purposes, as many industries are subject to regulations that mandate timely patching and reporting. Having a clear audit trail allows organizations to demonstrate their patch management efforts to regulatory bodies and auditors, reducing the risk of non-compliance fines. Additionally, tracking patching efforts enables organizations to verify that all systems are secure and that no devices are inadvertently left unpatched.

In highly dynamic environments, such as those using cloud-based VMs and containers, integrating patch management into the broader DevOps and continuous integration/continuous deployment (CI/CD) pipelines can also be beneficial. By embedding patching into the software development lifecycle, organizations can ensure that patches are applied as part of the deployment process. This integration helps to ensure that security vulnerabilities are addressed early in the development process and that patches are deployed automatically as part of the deployment of new features or updates to production environments.

While patching virtual machines and containers poses unique challenges, it also offers significant benefits in terms of system security, operational efficiency, and compliance. By automating the patching process, testing updates rigorously, and maintaining comprehensive tracking systems, organizations can ensure that their virtualized and containerized environments remain secure and up-to-date. The integration of patch management practices into the broader IT and development strategies further enhances the organization's ability to manage and mitigate risks associated with vulnerabilities in both virtual machines and containers. With the right systems in place, patching becomes not just a necessary task but an integral part of maintaining a resilient and secure IT infrastructure.

The Challenges of Patch Management in Fast-Moving Development Environments

In fast-moving development environments, where rapid deployment and frequent updates are the norm, patch management can become an especially complex and challenging task. Organizations that prioritize speed and agility in their software development processes often face a tension between the need to implement timely security patches and the demand for quick iterations, new features, and bug fixes. The fast-paced nature of development cycles can lead to overlooked vulnerabilities, delayed patch deployment, and difficulty in maintaining system stability. Balancing security with speed is essential in ensuring that patch management practices do not hinder development progress while simultaneously safeguarding systems and data from potential threats.

One of the primary challenges of patch management in fast-moving development environments is the sheer velocity of changes. Development teams often operate in short sprints, continuously pushing new code, features, and fixes to production. This rapid pace of change can make it difficult to implement and track patches effectively. Patches, which are released in response to identified security vulnerabilities or system issues, require thorough testing, validation, and deployment. In environments where new releases are frequent, the patching process can quickly become backlogged, leaving systems vulnerable. The constant updates and changes make it harder for IT and security teams to keep up with patching requirements, as each new release may introduce new vulnerabilities or require additional fixes that need to be prioritized. In such environments, security may take a backseat to speed, with patches either being delayed or applied inconsistently.

Additionally, the complexity of modern development environments further complicates patch management. With the widespread adoption of microservices, containerization, and cloud infrastructure, the landscape of patch management has become increasingly intricate. Microservices and containers introduce many small, independent services that are often updated independently of one another. This can make patch management difficult, as each service or containerized application may have its own patching requirements and schedules. Moreover, the interconnectedness of microservices means that a vulnerability in one service can potentially affect others, making patching even more urgent. Managing patches in such an environment requires a high level of coordination and oversight to ensure that all components are addressed and secured. Without proper patch management systems in place, development teams may inadvertently overlook certain services or fail to deploy critical updates in a timely manner, exposing the entire infrastructure to potential risks.

Another challenge in fast-moving development environments is the lack of clear visibility into the security status of all systems. In dynamic environments where developers continuously push new code and make changes to production systems, it becomes difficult for security and IT teams to maintain a real-time understanding of what systems are running, which versions are deployed, and where vulnerabilities exist. This lack of visibility can lead to confusion, as teams may not always be aware of what patches have been applied, which systems remain unpatched, or whether a recent release introduced new vulnerabilities. In such cases, patch management is often reactive rather than proactive, with teams scrambling to apply patches after a vulnerability has already been exploited or after a security breach has occurred. Organizations need comprehensive patch management tools that can offer real-time visibility into all systems and continuously monitor for vulnerabilities to ensure that patches are applied consistently and quickly.

The difficulty in coordinating patch management across different environments—such as development, staging, and production—also presents a significant hurdle in fast-moving development settings. Patches that work well in a development or staging environment may not perform as expected when deployed to production. Differences in configurations, software versions, and dependencies across environments can introduce unforeseen issues when patches are applied. In these environments, patch deployment must be carefully coordinated to avoid introducing new bugs or performance issues. However, testing patches in production is often impractical, as it can cause disruptions to users and services. As a result, many organizations rely on automated tools to test patches before deployment, but this only mitigates the problem rather than eliminating it altogether. Without effective coordination and thorough testing, patches that are applied too quickly can lead to system instability, which can disrupt development work and delay product launches.

Speed is a core principle in fast-moving development environments, often prioritized over security. This results in a tendency to adopt an "as needed" approach to patching—patches are applied when vulnerabilities are discovered or after an exploit occurs, rather than as part of a regular, proactive patch management strategy. As a result, security patches are often not applied until after a critical issue arises, leaving systems exposed to exploitation in the meantime. This reactive approach to patch management can result in costly data breaches, as organizations fail to patch known vulnerabilities that are actively targeted by attackers. In high-pressure environments, where the focus is often on new features and rapid product delivery, addressing patch management can be seen as secondary to the release of new products. However, this mindset only increases the risk of security incidents, which can have far-reaching consequences for both the organization and its customers.

In addition to the challenges posed by speed and complexity, resource constraints can further hinder effective patch management in fast-moving development environments. Small development teams or those with limited resources may struggle to allocate time and personnel to patching efforts. Developers may prioritize building new features or meeting deadlines over security tasks such as patching, leaving these efforts to IT or security teams who may already be overburdened. Additionally, organizations may lack the necessary tools or infrastructure to automate patch management processes, resulting in manual, time-consuming efforts to identify, test, and deploy patches across systems. This lack of resources can result in delayed patch deployment, increasing the likelihood of security vulnerabilities being exploited. Organizations must balance the need for speed with an investment in patch management tools and resources that can automate and streamline the patching process, freeing up teams to focus on development while maintaining a secure environment.

Lastly, communication and collaboration between development, operations, and security teams play a vital role in overcoming patch management challenges in fast-moving environments. In many organizations, patch management is siloed, with security and IT teams working independently of development teams. This lack of collaboration can lead to misunderstandings, delays, and inefficiencies in the patching process. For example, development teams may push new code that introduces vulnerabilities without being aware of patching requirements, or security teams may apply patches without informing developers of potential disruptions. To address this, organizations must foster a culture of collaboration between development, security, and IT operations. By working together, teams can ensure that patches are applied proactively, minimize disruptions, and keep systems secure while maintaining the speed and agility that development teams require.

In fast-moving development environments, patch management can seem like a daunting challenge, but it is an essential part of maintaining secure and reliable systems. By adopting proactive patch management strategies, automating patch deployment, improving visibility across environments, and fostering collaboration between teams, organizations can ensure that security does not take a backseat to speed. The key lies in balancing the need for agility with the responsibility to protect systems from vulnerabilities that could expose the organization to significant risks.

Best Practices for Patch Documentation and Reporting

Effective patch management is an essential element of an organization's cybersecurity strategy, ensuring that systems are protected from vulnerabilities and remain secure against cyber threats. However, a key but often overlooked aspect of patch management is the documentation and reporting of patching activities. Proper patch documentation and reporting not only ensure that patch management processes are carried out in a transparent and accountable manner but also play a crucial role in demonstrating compliance with industry regulations, auditing requirements, and internal security policies. To ensure that patch management is both efficient and effective, organizations must implement best practices for documenting and reporting patches, ensuring that they maintain an organized, clear, and accurate record of all patching activities.

One of the most important best practices for patch documentation is maintaining a centralized, comprehensive record of all patches applied to systems. This includes details about the patch itself, such as its release date, the vulnerabilities it addresses, the affected systems or applications, and the deployment status. Having a centralized record allows IT and security teams to track the progress of patching efforts across the entire organization, ensuring that no system is left unpatched and that all patches are applied in a timely manner. It also provides a reference for future patching efforts, enabling teams to identify recurring vulnerabilities or common issues that may require further investigation. Centralized documentation is especially important in large or complex environments where multiple systems, software versions, and patching methods are used. By keeping a detailed and accessible log of all patches, organizations can quickly assess the current state of their systems and make informed decisions about future patching needs.

In addition to recording basic patching information, organizations should document the rationale behind patching decisions. This includes the reasons for applying or delaying a patch, the potential impact of the patch, and the level of urgency associated with it. For example, if a critical vulnerability is identified and a patch is available, the organization should document the urgency of applying the patch and any mitigating steps taken if the patch cannot be applied immediately. Similarly, if a patch is delayed due to compatibility issues, the reasoning behind this decision should be clearly recorded, along with any workarounds or temporary solutions that have been implemented to mitigate the risk until the patch can be applied. By documenting the decision-making process, organizations ensure that patch management activities are carried out thoughtfully and strategically, rather than on an ad-hoc basis. This also provides transparency for audits or regulatory reviews, where the justification for patching actions may need to be demonstrated.

Another key practice in patch documentation is tracking the testing and validation process for patches. Before deploying patches to production systems, organizations should test them in controlled environments to verify their effectiveness and assess potential side effects, such as system crashes or compatibility issues. It is essential to document the results of these tests, including any issues discovered, the steps taken to resolve them, and the final outcome of the testing process. This documentation helps ensure that patches are deployed only after they have been thoroughly vetted and will not introduce new vulnerabilities or disrupt critical services. It also provides a historical record of testing efforts, which can be valuable when reviewing patching practices or troubleshooting issues that arise after patches are deployed. In high-stakes environments, such as healthcare or financial services, testing and validation documentation can be critical for ensuring compliance with industry regulations and maintaining service availability.

Regular reporting is another vital aspect of patch management. Effective reporting provides IT and security teams with visibility into the status of patching efforts, helping them identify areas where patches are overdue, incomplete, or not applied. Reporting can also highlight patterns or trends in patching activities, such as recurring vulnerabilities that require more in-depth remediation or patches that consistently cause compatibility issues. Reports should be generated regularly—ideally on a weekly or monthly basis—to track patch deployment progress and ensure that all systems are up-to-date. These reports should include key metrics, such as the percentage of systems patched, the number of critical patches applied, the number of unpatched systems, and the average time taken to apply patches. By regularly reviewing these reports, organizations can identify areas for improvement, adjust their patching strategies, and ensure that their patch management efforts align with organizational security goals.

Furthermore, reporting on patch management should be tailored to different stakeholders, with varying levels of detail depending on the audience. For example, IT and security teams may require detailed reports with technical data, such as the specifics of each patch, its installation status, and any testing or validation results. Executives or upper management, on the other hand, may need high-level reports that focus on overall patching progress, risk assessments, and the organization's compliance with relevant regulations. Tailoring patch management reports to the needs of different stakeholders ensures that the right information is communicated to the right people in an efficient and actionable manner. For example, an executive report might focus on the number of high-risk vulnerabilities patched in the past quarter, while a technical report for IT teams would include details of each individual patch and its status across all systems.

In addition to internal documentation and reporting, organizations should also consider external reporting requirements for regulatory compliance and audits. Many industries, such as healthcare, finance, and government, are subject to strict regulations that require organizations to maintain detailed records of their patch management activities. For instance, the Health Insurance Portability and Accountability Act (HIPAA) in the United States mandates that healthcare organizations apply security patches promptly to protect patient data, and they must be able to demonstrate this through documentation. Similarly, organizations in the financial sector must comply with the Payment Card Industry Data Security Standard (PCI DSS), which includes requirements for patching known vulnerabilities to protect cardholder data. External auditors may review patch management documentation to verify compliance with these regulations, so it is crucial that organizations maintain accurate and comprehensive records that can be easily accessed and reviewed when necessary.

To facilitate effective patch documentation and reporting, organizations should implement automated patch management tools. These tools can help track patches, monitor deployment status, and generate reports without the need for manual data entry. Automation reduces the risk of human error and ensures that documentation is consistently updated in real-time. Additionally, automated tools can integrate with existing IT management systems, providing a unified view of patching efforts across the entire organization. This integration streamlines the patch management process and helps ensure that all relevant data is captured and reported accurately.

Maintaining comprehensive patch documentation and reporting is a vital aspect of a strong patch management program. Clear, organized records of patching activities enable organizations to demonstrate compliance, assess the effectiveness of their patch management efforts, and make data-driven decisions about future patching priorities. Effective reporting provides transparency and visibility into patching progress, helping organizations identify potential weaknesses, prioritize critical patches, and ensure that systems remain secure. By adopting best practices for patch documentation and reporting, organizations can build a solid foundation for ongoing patch management and strengthen their overall cybersecurity posture.

The Future of Patch Management: Trends and Innovations

Patch management has long been a cornerstone of maintaining cybersecurity and system integrity in organizations. As technology continues to evolve at a rapid pace, so too do the methods and tools used for patch management. The landscape of patch management is undergoing significant transformations as businesses increasingly adopt new technologies, such as cloud computing, containerization, artificial intelligence (AI), and machine learning (ML). These advancements not only change the way patching is done but also introduce new challenges and opportunities for enhancing the effectiveness and efficiency of patch management practices. Looking to the future, several trends and innovations are poised to reshape the patch management process, making it more automated, intelligent, and adaptable to the growing complexity of modern IT environments.

One of the most prominent trends shaping the future of patch management is the increasing automation of patch deployment. As the number of devices and systems that require patching continues to grow, manually managing patches across a wide array of environments becomes increasingly untenable. Automation tools, which can schedule, test, and deploy patches without human intervention, are rapidly becoming a staple of modern IT operations. These tools use predefined rules and policies to identify systems that need patching, schedule updates, and even roll back patches if necessary. The integration of automation in patch management reduces the risk of human error, accelerates the deployment process, and ensures that patches are applied consistently across the entire infrastructure. In the future, automation will become even more sophisticated, with systems able to dynamically adapt to the specific needs of individual systems and environments. This will enable patching processes to occur seamlessly and without disruption, ensuring that systems remain secure and operational at all times.

Alongside automation, artificial intelligence and machine learning are playing an increasingly important role in the evolution of patch management. AI and ML have the potential to revolutionize patch management by making it smarter and more predictive. Rather than relying solely on reactive patching methods, where patches are applied after vulnerabilities are discovered, AI can analyze patterns in data, identify potential risks, and predict when and where vulnerabilities are likely to emerge. By leveraging vast amounts of data from threat intelligence feeds, past vulnerabilities, and historical patching efforts, AI systems can prioritize patches based on their severity and exploitability. Machine learning algorithms can also improve the accuracy of patch testing, reducing the likelihood that patches will cause unintended side effects or system outages. As AI continues to evolve, it will enable organizations to proactively address vulnerabilities before they are exploited, thereby reducing the overall risk of security breaches.

Another trend shaping the future of patch management is the growing importance of patching in complex IT environments, particularly in cloud-native architectures and containerized applications. The adoption of cloud computing and containerization has significantly changed how software is deployed, scaled, and maintained. In these environments, systems are often distributed across multiple locations, and workloads are constantly being spun up or torn down. This dynamic and ephemeral nature of cloud and containerized environments presents unique challenges for patch management. The future of patch management will need to account for these complexities by developing solutions that can scale across cloud environments, manage containerized applications, and handle the unique patching requirements of microservices-based architectures. Tools that can automatically patch containers as they are created and destroyed, while ensuring consistency across distributed environments, will become essential for organizations adopting cloud-native technologies. As more organizations embrace these technologies, patch management will need to evolve to ensure that security is maintained without sacrificing the agility that cloud and containerized environments offer.

Furthermore, the future of patch management will involve greater integration with DevOps and continuous integration/continuous deployment (CI/CD) pipelines. DevOps practices, which emphasize collaboration between development and operations teams to streamline the software development lifecycle, have already revolutionized the way software is built and deployed. As organizations continue to embrace DevOps, patch management will need to be integrated into the development pipeline, ensuring that security patches are applied as part of the continuous deployment process. This means that patches will not only be applied to production systems but also tested and validated in development and staging environments before they are released. The integration of patch management into CI/CD pipelines will enable faster and more reliable patching, as well as ensure that patches are applied without disrupting development or operational workflows. In the future, automated patching will be a seamless part of the CI/CD process, enabling developers to focus on building new features while maintaining the security of their applications.

A key innovation in patch management that is likely to gain traction in the future is the use of blockchain technology for ensuring patch integrity and authenticity. One of the challenges with patch management today is ensuring that patches are authentic and have not been tampered with. With the increasing number of cyberattacks targeting the patching process itself, organizations need a way to verify that patches are legitimate and have been applied correctly. Blockchain technology offers a secure, decentralized way to record patching activities, providing an immutable record of all patches applied to a system. By leveraging blockchain, organizations can ensure that patches are not altered or compromised during deployment, and they can trace the entire patching history of a system. This can be particularly useful in highly regulated industries, where the authenticity and integrity of patches are critical for compliance with standards like HIPAA or PCI DSS.

Additionally, patch management is expected to become more integrated with broader security operations. In the future, patching will not be seen as a standalone process but as an integral part of an organization's overall cybersecurity strategy. As the attack surface continues to grow and cyber threats become more sophisticated, patch management will be closely linked with threat intelligence, vulnerability management, and incident response. Patch management systems will work in tandem with security operations centers (SOCs), automatically feeding information about vulnerabilities, exploits, and patched systems into the organization's broader security monitoring efforts. This integration will enable faster response times to emerging threats, as security teams will be able to quickly identify unpatched systems that are vulnerable to active exploits. Additionally, by linking patch management with broader security measures, organizations can ensure that their patching efforts are aligned with their overall security posture and that they are addressing vulnerabilities in a timely and comprehensive manner.

As patch management continues to evolve, so too will the tools and technologies used to support it. The future will likely see greater use of cloud-based patch management solutions that provide centralized control and visibility across diverse and distributed environments. These cloud-based platforms will allow organizations to manage patches across a wide range of systems, applications, and devices, without being limited by geographical or infrastructure constraints. Additionally, cloud-based solutions will enable patch management systems to scale more easily, adapting to the increasing complexity and volume of patches as organizations grow and diversify their IT environments.

The future of patch management is undoubtedly shaped by ongoing technological advancements. From the increased use of automation, AI, and machine learning to the integration with DevOps, blockchain technology, and cloud-based solutions, the landscape of patch management is set to become more efficient, secure, and agile. These innovations will help organizations not only keep up with the growing volume and complexity of patches but also ensure that their systems remain secure and resilient against an ever-evolving threat landscape. As patch management continues to evolve, organizations must adapt to these changes and invest in the technologies and practices that will help them stay ahead of emerging threats and maintain robust security across their IT environments.

Continuous Improvement in Patch Management Strategies

In today's rapidly evolving digital landscape, cybersecurity is an ever-present concern. Organizations must adapt quickly to a variety of challenges, from newly discovered vulnerabilities to emerging threats and constantly changing technology. Patch management plays a critical role in maintaining the security and stability of IT environments. It involves identifying, testing, and deploying patches for software and systems to fix vulnerabilities, improve performance, and address bugs. However, patch management is not a one-time task but a continuous process that requires constant refinement. Ensuring that patch management strategies evolve over time is key to maintaining a resilient security posture and minimizing potential risks to the organization.

The concept of continuous improvement in patch management strategies is rooted in the idea that patching should not be seen as a static, isolated activity but as an ongoing, dynamic process. As new vulnerabilities are discovered, software updates are released, and business priorities shift, patch management strategies must evolve to keep pace. The first step in implementing continuous improvement is establishing a structured framework for patch management. This framework should be flexible enough to allow for adjustments as the IT landscape changes, ensuring that patch management efforts align with the organization's broader security goals. A well-defined framework helps teams stay organized, prioritize tasks, and track progress over time.

One important aspect of continuous improvement in patch management is developing an agile approach to vulnerability management. In the past, many organizations took a reactive approach to patching, waiting for vendors to release patches before applying them to their systems. This approach is increasingly inadequate in today's fast-paced cybersecurity environment. Attackers are constantly searching for unpatched vulnerabilities, and delays in patch deployment can lead to severe security breaches. To address this, organizations must adopt a proactive stance, continuously scanning for vulnerabilities, identifying risks in real-time, and applying patches as soon as they become available. Continuous vulnerability scanning tools can automatically detect missing patches, assess their risk levels, and prioritize remediation efforts based on the severity of the vulnerabilities.

Another essential element of continuous improvement is the integration of patch management with other cybersecurity processes, such as risk management, incident response, and compliance monitoring. Patch management cannot operate in isolation if it is to be effective. Integrating it with other aspects of the organization's security framework ensures that patches are applied in alignment with broader security objectives and that any risks or vulnerabilities are addressed in a timely manner. For example, incident response teams must be alerted when critical vulnerabilities are discovered and patches are needed to mitigate the risk of an exploit. Similarly, compliance requirements often dictate how quickly patches should be applied, especially in regulated industries such as healthcare and finance. A collaborative, cross-functional approach allows organizations to respond more swiftly to threats and ensures that patch management efforts are not hindered by siloed processes.

Automation plays a key role in the continuous improvement of patch management strategies. With the increasing number of software applications, operating systems, and devices that organizations rely on, manually managing patches can become a daunting and error-prone task. Automation tools can streamline the patching process by automatically identifying missing patches, scheduling patch deployments, and ensuring that patches are applied consistently across the organization's entire IT infrastructure. These tools can also help with testing patches in non-production environments, reducing the likelihood of compatibility issues or system downtime. By automating routine tasks, organizations can free up valuable resources and allow their IT teams to focus on more strategic activities, such as improving security protocols and identifying emerging threats.

However, automation is not a silver bullet, and continuous improvement in patch management also requires robust monitoring and reporting systems. Simply automating patch deployments is not enough if the results are not properly tracked and analyzed. Monitoring systems must be in place to ensure that patches are being applied correctly and that systems remain secure. Regular reporting provides visibility into the patching process, offering detailed insights into which patches have been applied, which are still pending, and any issues that have arisen during deployment. These reports can also help identify trends in patch management, such as recurring delays or vulnerabilities that frequently require fixes. By continuously monitoring patching activities and generating detailed reports, organizations can track their progress, identify areas for improvement, and ensure compliance with internal and external security standards.

As part of the continuous improvement process, organizations should also emphasize the importance of ongoing training and education for their IT teams. Patch management strategies and technologies are constantly evolving, and keeping staff up to date on the latest tools, techniques, and best practices is essential. Regular training helps teams understand new security threats, learn how to work with new patching technologies, and stay informed about changes in regulatory requirements. Additionally, educating teams about the importance of patch management and fostering a culture of security awareness helps ensure that patching is treated as a priority rather than an afterthought. Engaged, well-informed teams are better equipped to manage patching processes efficiently and respond to emerging security threats quickly.

Feedback loops are another key component of continuous improvement in patch management. After patches are applied, it is important to assess their effectiveness in mitigating the vulnerabilities they were designed to fix. This can involve conducting vulnerability scans, penetration testing, or other forms of security validation to verify that the patch has resolved the issue without introducing new problems. Feedback from these assessments should be used to inform future patch management decisions. For example, if a particular patch causes system instability or conflicts with other software, this information can be used to improve testing procedures and prevent similar issues in the future. By establishing a feedback loop, organizations can ensure that their patch management processes are constantly evolving based on real-world experiences and outcomes.

Collaboration with external vendors and partners is another important aspect of continuous improvement. Many software vendors release patches regularly to address security vulnerabilities, but the speed at which they release these updates can vary. For critical patches, organizations need to be able to quickly apply updates as soon as they become available. Effective communication with vendors ensures that organizations are promptly informed of new patches and updates, and it also allows them to collaborate on testing and troubleshooting if any issues arise after a patch is deployed. By maintaining strong relationships with vendors and staying informed about their patch release cycles, organizations can ensure that their patch management processes are aligned with the latest security best practices.

The evolving nature of cybersecurity threats means that patch management strategies must be continuously adapted to address new risks and challenges. As organizations grow and their IT environments become more complex, patch management processes must evolve to remain effective. Leveraging new technologies, such as artificial intelligence and machine learning, will help organizations predict vulnerabilities, automate patching, and prioritize patches more efficiently. Emphasizing continuous improvement in patch management practices ensures that organizations remain resilient to evolving cyber threats, can quickly adapt to new challenges, and can maintain a high level of security across their entire IT infrastructure.

Continuous improvement in patch management is an ongoing effort that requires organizations to be proactive, agile, and adaptable. By integrating automation, monitoring, feedback, and collaboration into their patch management strategies, organizations can ensure that they are effectively managing vulnerabilities and staying ahead of emerging threats. With the right approach, patch management becomes a crucial component of an organization's broader security strategy, helping to protect sensitive data, maintain system integrity, and ensure business continuity.

www.ingramcontent.com/pod-product-compliance
Lightning Source LLC
LaVergne TN
LVHW022314060326
832902LV00020B/3457